CHANGING CLIMATES

GL🌐BAL C🌐NNECTI🌐NS

GLOBAL CONNECTIONS

CHANGING CLIMATES

CHARLES F. GRITZNER

This book is lovingly dedicated to Janalyce Ham Taylor, the most wonderful sister with whom anyone could ever be blessed. As a believer in the threat of global warming, she asked—a doubter with an open, inquiring mind. Jan's interest, along with that of many others who are deeply concerned about the future of our planet and humanity, provided the inspiration for writing this book.

Changing Climates

Copyright © 2010 by Infobase Publishing

Chelsea House
An imprint of Infobase Publishing
132 West 31st Street
New York, NY 10001

Library of Congress Cataloging-in-Publication Data
Gritzner, Charles F.
 Changing climates / by Charles F. Gritzner.
  p. cm. — (Global connections)
 Includes bibliographical references and index.
 ISBN 978-1-60413-291-5 (hardcover : alk. paper) 1. Global warming—Juvenile literature. 2. Climatic changes—Juvenile literature. 3. Climatic changes—History—Juvenile literature. 4. Nature—Effect of human beings on—Juvenile literature. 5. Global warming—Government policy—Juvenile literature. I. Title. II. Series.
 QC981.8.G56G75 2009
 363.738'74—dc22   2009033603

Chelsea House books are available at special discounts when purchased in bulk quantities for businesses, associations, institutions, or sales promotions. Please call our Special Sales Department in New York at (212) 967-8800 or (800) 322-8755.

You can find Chelsea House on the World Wide Web
at http://www.chelseahouse.com

Text design by Annie O'Donnell
Cover design by Takeshi Takahashi
Composition by EJB Publishing Services
Cover printed by Bang Printing, Brainerd, MN
Book printed and bound by Bang Printing, Brainerd, MN
Date printed: June 2010
Printed in the United States of America

10 9 8 7 6 5 4 3 2 1

This book is printed on acid-free paper.

All links and Web addresses were checked and verified to be correct at the time of publication. Because of the dynamic nature of the Web, some addresses and links may have changed since publication and may no longer be valid.

CONTENTS

A GLOBAL COMMUNITY

Globalization is the process of coming together as a closely connected global community. It began thousands of years ago, when tribal groups and small hunting parties wandered from place to place. The process accelerated following Columbus's epic voyage more than five centuries ago. Europeans—an estimated 50 million of them—spread out to occupy lands throughout the world. This migration transformed the distribution of the world's peoples and their cultures forever. In the United States and Canada, for example, most people speak a West European language. Most practice a religious faith with roots in the ancient Middle East and eat foods originating in Asia.

Today, we are citizens of a closely interwoven global community. Events occurring half a world away can be watched and experienced, often as they happen, in our own homes. People, materials, and even diseases can be transported from continent to continent in a single day, thanks to jet planes. Electronic communications make possible the instantaneous exchange of information by phone, e-mail, or other means with friends or business associates almost anywhere in the world. Trade and commerce, perhaps more so than any other aspect of our daily lives, amply illustrate the importance of global linkages. How many things in your home (including your clothing) are of international origin? What foods and beverages have you consumed today that came from other lands? Could Northern America's economy survive without foreign oil, iron ore, copper, or other vital resources?

The GLOBAL CONNECTIONS series is designed to help you realize how closely people and places are tied to one another within the expanding global community. Each book introduces you to political, economic, environmental, social, medical, and other timely issues, problems, and prospects. The authors and editors hope you enjoy and learn from these books. May they hand you a passport to intellectual travels throughout our fascinating, complex, and increasingly "intradependent" world!

—*Charles F. Gritzner*
Series Editor

INTRODUCTION TO CLIMATE CHANGE

Climates change. They have changed throughout Earth's history, and they will continue to change. Some changes are short-term, lasting only a matter of years or decades. Others last for hundreds, thousands, or even millions of years. When they occur, much of Earth's surface can be turned into a frigid, ice-covered wasteland. On other occasions, temperatures soar to levels that are much warmer than today. When the planet warms, conditions favor lush vegetation. With an ample food supply, animals thrive, such as happened during the era of dinosaurs. Like a swinging pendulum, colder and warmer climates come and go. Their rhythmic changes are caused by various natural cycles. Many factors contribute to both short- and long-term atmospheric changes. Scientists now understand many, although not all, causes of changing weather and climate.

(Note: Historians often limit use of the word *history*, or *historical*, to the documented, or written, past. Events that occurred before that time are left to archaeologists, geologists, or other scientists who study features and conditions that existed long before people began to write. For our purposes, *history* refers to past events regardless of how long ago they occurred.)

CLIMATE AND CONTROVERSY

During recent decades a new dimension has been added to the debate over climate change. Many people, including some scientists, believe that humans, in addition to various natural agents, are causing weather, hence climate, to change. This is the increasingly heated debate over what some people believe to be catastrophic anthropogenic global warming (AGW). They believe that human activity is causing global temperatures to warm at an alarming rate. Burning of carbon dioxide–releasing fossil fuels (coal, petroleum, and natural gas), they argue, is the primary cause of warming.

Understanding climate change is a matter that should be left to responsible scientists. Unfortunately, it is an issue that has moved far beyond the limits of scientific study and analysis. In many respects, the global warming debate has turned into a bitter free-for-all. Flames of controversy are fueled by an opportunistic media. And they are fanned by interests promoting their own economic, social, and political agendas. Meanwhile, most citizens lack the scientific knowledge to judge the merits of various sides of the issue. Therefore, their opinions are based upon what they see, read, and hear. And those sources of information are often very biased, non-scientific, and unreliable.

Many people base their climate-related beliefs on emotion and "faith"-based convictions. In the absence of scientific understanding, what should be a serious and reasoned debate has been turned into a three-ring circus. Former U.S. vice president Al Gore, for example, was awarded the coveted Nobel Peace Prize and two Academy Awards for his efforts to bring attention to global warming. Yet his very controversial media presentation strays far from scientific reality. Most literature on global warming is highly polarized: That is, in a very biased way it takes a strong stand one way or another in regard to the issue. Throughout this book, the author will present what he believes to be honest evidence. It will be left to *you* to decide what is or is not happening and why in regard to changing climates.

WEATHER VERSUS CLIMATE

Weather is the day-to-day condition of the atmosphere. It is what is happening *now* in a particular place. If you go outside, how many different atmospheric conditions can you identify? Is the temperature hot, warm, cool, or cold? Is precipitation falling in the form of rain, snow, hail, or sleet? Finally, can you feel wind, the movement of air from areas of high pressure to areas of low pressure?

Climate is the long-term average condition of the weather. On a particular day, it may be cool and rainy someplace in the desert Southwest of the United States. That describes today's weather. Year in and year out, however, the region is warm and dry. Therefore, it is classified as having a subtropical desert climate. An area of the Deep South may be gripped by severe drought, and mid-winter temperatures may drop below freezing for several days. But the region is usually moist and relatively warm; hence, it experiences a humid subtropical climate.

How many changes in weather can you think of during a day? A year? A longer period? Has your area experienced any major shifts in weather during recent years? For example, has it become wetter or drier? Have summers or winters become warmer or cooler? Does your area show evidence of a much different climate in times past? (For example, 90 percent of all natural lakes were formed by glacial action.) Conduct research to learn more about past climatic conditions in your area.

UNDERSTANDING CLIMATE CHANGE

Climate change is nothing new. Geographical evidence shows it has been a part of Earth's long history. For example, during the Ice Age, eastern South Dakota was buried beneath a huge sheet of glacial ice, perhaps a mile deep. In the western part of the state, various fossil remains suggest a vastly different climatic story. They offer evidence of the region having been much warmer than it is today.

Major changes in climate have also occurred during recent history. Between about A.D. 1000 and 1300, temperatures were considerably warmer than those today. This, of course, was centuries before automobiles and air-fouling industries began to spew carbon dioxide (CO_2) into the atmosphere. During this time, called the Medieval Warm Period, Greenlanders raised wheat along the fringe of the island's shrinking ice sheet.

A century later, by 1400, temperatures had plunged. Conditions were so cold throughout Europe and elsewhere in the Northern Hemisphere that the period is called the Little Ice Age. For nearly 500 years glaciers advanced, and many normally ice-free lakes, rivers, and harbors froze over for the first time in memory. In what is now the United States, Spanish explorers described extremely cold weather conditions. Francisco Coronado spent two winters in the Upper Rio Grande Valley of present-day New Mexico during the early 1540s. He reported that the river froze over for several months at a time, something that has not happened since. Similar reports of extreme cold and deep snow were given by Hernando de Soto and other Spaniards exploring areas of the present-day southeastern United States.

More recently, from the mid-1960s through the mid-1980s, temperatures were quite cool. During this period, in fact, many scientists were concerned that Earth was entering another ice age! Today, of course, the concern is over what some believe to be a condition of global warming.

Fossils in Badlands National Park in South Dakota provide clues to the climate in the area millions of years ago. During its history, Earth's climate has changed considerably, swinging from one extreme to another, and everything in between.

Understanding climate change is a question that involves experts from many different sciences. Most directly, the study of atmospheric sciences involves the work of meteorologists (scientists who study weather) and climatologists (those who study climates). But many other scientists are deeply involved in the study of weather and climate and their importance. Geographers focus upon the spatial patterns of climatic conditions. They are interested in learning what is happening where, why conditions are occurring there, and why we should care about weather and climate.

Geologists use rocks, fossils, and other clues to determine past climatic conditions, often going back millions of years.

Botanists, zoologists, and pedologists (soil scientists) share an interest in climate change. So do ecologists, hydrologists, and many other physical scientists. Basically, all of them want to know what effect changing climates have upon other natural environmental conditions.

Many social scientists are also interested in climatic change. The anthropologist and archaeologist study how different cultures adapt to changes in temperature and moisture. Economists certainly are interested in the effect of climate on various economic activities. Sociologists and psychologists might study the impact of environmental change on societies and on human well-being. Historians are interested in how climate change affected human activities and institutions in the past.

HUMANS AND CLIMATE

Archaeological evidence suggests that some early humans lived at the very edge of the vast continental ice sheets. More recently, about 30,000 years ago, humans were surviving in northeastern Siberia and bitterly cold, ice-free areas of northern Europe. Early wanderers in search of game may even have crossed the frigid Bering Strait region from Asia into North America.

If properly dressed and equipped, humans can survive severe cold. The Inuit (Eskimo) have lived comfortably in far northern areas of North America and Greenland for several thousand years. Today, as in times past, people have also occupied the world's hottest places. In fact, evidence suggests that humans (*Homo sapiens*) began their life journey in the equatorial tropics of East Africa. Biologically, we are tropical animals with bodies adapted to warmth. When unprotected, our bodies begin to experience hypothermia (a life-threatening reaction to the cold) when temperatures drop below 77°F (25°C).

Today nearly 2 billion people live in tropical and subtropical areas. Temperatures in the tropical zone average 20 to 40 degrees higher than in most of the middle latitudes. So, one might logically ask, "What is to be feared from a several-degree rise in temperature?" Would it be catastrophic for temperatures to rise a few degrees in the cooler middle latitudes and polar regions? It is there, after all, that most of the rise in temperature is occurring.

If humans are physically adapted to a warm environment, how can our presence in many extremely cold locations (including research stations on Antarctica) be explained? The answer is culture, which is humankind's adaptive mechanism. All other life forms are biologically adapted to the environments in which they live. They are born with certain physical characteristics that restrict them to a particular habitat (the environment in which an organism can survive). It is impossible for them to survive outside of that environment. Humans, like other life-forms, have physical limits. But culture allows us to vastly expand our habitat. Be thankful for such things as insulated structures, warm clothing, and artificial heating. Without them, we would still be living in the equatorial tropics!

WHAT LIES AHEAD?

In the following text, we attempt to address three important questions. First, is Earth's temperature really warming and, if so, is it warming at an alarming rate? Second, if warming is occurring, is it caused by human activity? That is, are recent climatic changes anthropogenic in origin or are they in response to natural cycles? Finally, would many of the proposed responses to global warming be effective? If not, what might happen if they were adopted?

This book attempts to explain climatic change both historically and in terms of present concerns and future prospects. In the following chapter, you will learn how climate has changed through time. You will see that historically Earth's climate has been either much warmer or much colder than today. Such extremes, in fact, are far more common than is the present relatively mild global climate. Chapter 3 focuses upon the causes of climate change. It explains the ways in which the sun, land and water surfaces, and the atmosphere itself influence Earth's temperatures. In Chapter 4, you will find out how a change of climate influences most, if not all, other elements of the natural environment. Chapters 5, 6, and 7 focus upon present-day concerns over climate change, with emphasis on anthropogenic global warming. In the final chapter, we will look to the future and what it may hold for climate change and its impact on the human condition.

CLIMATE CHANGE THROUGH TIME

Climate is like a roller coaster. Temperatures (and other weather elements) can and do change dramatically. When millions of years of temperature change is plotted on a graph, the periods of high and low temperatures resemble the high peaks, steep plunges, and sharp turns of a thrilling ride. And as anyone who ever has ridden a roller coaster knows, the rises, turns, and drops can occur suddenly and unexpectedly. The same is true of climate.

Many major changes in climate, of course, happened long before the dawn of humankind. To better understand the age of Earth versus that of humans, imagine the history of our planet represented by 24 hours on a clock. How long do you think humans have been around? Following the 24-hour example, in even our most primitive and ancient form, we have existed for less than five minutes! And as *Homo sapiens* (meaning "wise man"), we have been on the planet for less than one minute. As modern humans—similar to today's population in physical features—we have existed only a few seconds. Clearly, most climate changes did not affect humans because we were not around. Therefore, we will pay most attention to climate changes that have occurred during the several million years of human history.

As you will learn, humans have survived an amazing number of often abrupt changes in weather and climate. And many of them were extreme in their effect upon humans and all other life-forms. Again, it is important to remember that at times large areas of Earth's surface experienced temperatures that were much warmer than they are today. At other times, large portions of the middle and higher latitudes were buried beneath huge sheets of glacial ice.

MEASURING CLIMATE CHANGE

Reliable methods for measuring temperatures are a relatively recent development. The thermometer (from *thermo,* meaning "temperature," and *meter,* "to measure") is the instrument used to measure temperature. It evolved slowly over a period of many centuries. However, highly accurate measurement of temperature and scales by which temperatures can be recorded are relatively recent developments. The reliable thermometer that uses mercury within a glass tube was created during the early eighteenth century.

About the same time, reliable scales by which measured temperatures could be standardized were developed. A German physicist, Daniel Fahrenheit, made the first mercury thermometer. He also created the temperature scale that bears his name. In the Fahrenheit scale, 32° is freezing and 212° is the boiling point of water. During the same time period, a Swedish astronomer, Anders Celsius, developed the scale identified with his name (it also is called centigrade). In the Celsius scale, 0° is the freezing point and 100° the boiling point of water under normal conditions. Methods to measure precipitation have existed for several millennia. Each culture that had a mathematical system created its own way to measure and record amounts of moisture.

SURROGATE RECORDS

A surrogate (or proxy) is anything that takes the place of something else. Modern thermometers and rain gauges can't reconstruct paleo (ancient) climates. Therefore, scientists who study paleoclimatology must rely upon surrogate indicators of climate change. Because weather and climate affect nearly all other natural elements, they have plenty of evidence to which they can turn. Since no one was around to experience early climates, many of their conclusions are based on informed guesswork.

Land Features

Many geologists study the impact of paleoclimates on various land features. Certain landforms, such as glaciated features, provide clues to the climatic conditions under which they were created. Some rock types, such as limestone and sandstone, can also provide clues to ancient climatic conditions. Geologists also use various fossil remains to reconstruct paleoclimates. There are other clues. Climate is a chief factor contributing to the weathering (breaking down), erosion (transportation), and deposition of rock material. The fossil fuels—coal, petroleum, and natural gas—formed during long periods when plant and animal life was much more abundant than it is today. This, for example, suggests climatic conditions that were very favorable to living organisms. In these and other much more complex ways, Earth scientists are able to "read" the history of Earth's changing climates.

Let's look at a specific example. In many places rocks are strewn about that do not match those that belong in the area. How did they get there? The U.S. Midwest is littered with glacial till, deposits that include rocks not native to the region. Southward-moving glaciers scooped up the material. They then deposited the earthen debris in a band that extends from north of the Missouri and Ohio rivers eastward into New England. This landscape, northward to the Arctic Ocean, is also dotted with millions of lakes. An estimated 90 percent of all lakes occupy basins that were scoured by glaciers. They include the Great Lakes of the United States and Canada. Such features provide ample proof of much colder conditions.

MAKING CONNECTIONS

THE CLIMATIC "ACCORDION"

Earth's climates are divided into many types. The number of climates, the conditions on which they are based, and the names by which they are identified vary greatly. Most of them reflect temperature and moisture, or a combination of the two elements. The tropical equatorial zone is hot and wet. Polar areas are extremely cold and dry. Elsewhere, climates fall somewhere in between the two extremes.

What happens when Earth's temperatures warm or cool? Do some climates disappear? Are new climatic regions formed? The answer is no. Rather, much like an accordion, they expand or contract in area. During cold periods, northern and southern polar climates spread into the middle latitudes. Mid-latitude and tropical climates contract, or shrink in size, as they are forced toward the equator. As temperatures warm, polar climates begin to contract and retreat toward the poles. This allows the equatorial and mid-latitude climatic zones to shift poleward and expand in area.

What would happen to Canada, the northern United States, and much of northern Eurasia if the global climate warmed (or cooled)? Do some research to find out what conditions are like in the climatic zones lying to the north and south of the one in which you live. Let's assume that you spend your lifetime in the same area in which you live today. What are some of the changes you would experience if either of your neighboring climates expanded to your location?

Biological Evidence

Fossils also provide many surrogate indices of past climates. All organisms are biologically limited in terms of their habitat. Paleontologists are scientists who study prehistoric plant and animal life in order to reconstruct the geologic (including climate) past. Basically, they study fossils to determine, among other things, the spatial distribution of ancient organisms. Once this information is known, they can reconstruct the environment in which an organism lived. In this way, by knowing the habitat in which a certain now fossilized plant or animal lived, ancient climatic conditions can be reconstructed. Coral reefs also reflect growth patterns that are influenced by climate. As a result, they, too, can provide valuable clues to earlier atmospheric conditions.

Certain conditions of weather and climate contribute to different growth rates in trees. In environments that experience seasonal changes of weather, trees develop annual growth rings. Perhaps you have seen the cross section of a tree trunk and counted the rings to determine the age of the tree. If so, you may have noticed that some rings were much wider than others. Wide rings represent a period of time during which conditions were favorable for growth. Weather was warm and moisture was adequate. Narrow rings show hard times, such as unusual cold or drought, which hindered tree growth. Using tree rings, dendrochronologists (tree ring scientists) can reconstruct changes in weather and climate over time. For some areas of the world, tree ring data exist for a period of more than 20,000 years before present (YBP). For most of the world, however, the tree ring calendar is much more limited. The bristlecone pine, found in California's White Mountains and various locations in Nevada, provides tree ring (and therefore climatic) data going back about 10,000 years.

Other Clues

Palynologists can also determine past climates by studying ancient pollen. Each plant is adapted to a particular environment and produces distinct pollen. By identifying pollen, plant types can be identified. Because their habitat is known, past climatic conditions can be reconstructed.

Annual changes in weather can also contribute to certain conditions that create layering. Sediments formed by various materials deposited on the ocean floor have accumulated over millions of years. When cored, they can reveal clues to past climatic conditions. Many mid- and high-latitude lake bottom sediments also are stratified with annually deposited layers. These layers, called varves, show light and dark bands. Light layers represent summer deposits, and dark layers are winter deposits, when sedimentation is reduced. Each combined layer, then, represents one year. The width of bands and the comparative size of light and dark markers over time indicate historical changes in climatic conditions.

In Greenland and Antarctica, glaciers can be cored. Cores show annual accumulations of snow as bands of varying width. In polar lands, glaciers grow or contract in response to the amount of snow that falls. Snowfall, in turn, is closely tied to temperature conditions. The mass of ice and length of glacial lobes (arms) also reveal changes in temperature and ice accumulation.

A HISTORY OF CHANGING CLIMATES

Earth is believed to be about 4.5 billion years old. For the purpose of our discussion, however, our story of changing climates begins with the dawn of early life around 3 billion years ago. Fossil remains of early plants and animals found in rock layers provide us with some of the oldest clues to ancient climates and climate change. Using methods discussed above (and many others), paleoclimatologists have developed a fairly detailed history of Earth's climates.

Throughout history, the planet's temperature has changed repeatedly. It has done so in various cycles (See Figure 1). Paleoclimatologists call these cycles "hot house," when warmer than average temperatures prevail, and "ice house," when temperatures are colder than average. You might be surprised to learn that today's temperatures are cooler than the historical average. They are, however, much warmer than those of the Ice Age that ended about 11,000 years ago. It is extremely important to remember that temperatures are relative. That is, conditions are hotter or colder than those during some previous time that is being used as a point of reference.

In terms of today's global warming debate, we must consider those conditions with which present temperatures are being compared. The points of reference from which today's warming trend is measured are periods of unusual cold. About 11,500 years before present (YBP), our planet began to thaw out from the frigid grip of the Ice Age (Pleistocene epoch). More recently, much of the Northern Hemisphere experienced the Little Ice Age, a frigid period that lasted from about 1300 to 1800. And several decades ago temperatures were so cold that many scientists were predicting another ice age.

Based upon these three periods, today's temperatures are warming. Conditions are many degrees warmer than when much of the Northern Hemisphere was buried beneath huge sheets of glacial ice. They are also much warmer than during the period of frigid conditions that brought misery and death to millions of people just a few short centuries ago. And compared to temperatures of 30 to 50 years ago, recent temperatures are considerably warmer. Based upon historical patterns, current temperature should be warming.

Earth has undergone several long periods during which temperatures were much colder than today. While experiencing ice house conditions, much land at high elevation and poleward latitudes was deeply buried beneath vast sheets of glacial ice. Our planet was locked in their icy grip for millions of years. Earth's recent average surface temperature is about 59°F (15°C). Since 1998, annual temperatures have been around 58°F (14.4°C), or about 1°F (0.6°C) lower than average each year. During periods of ice house conditions, temperatures averaged 7° to 9°F colder (4 to 5°C) than today. Huge portions of the world were unable to support plant or animal (including human) life.

History of Earth's Changing Climates
Today
1.8 million 11,500 YBP
65 million– 1.8 million YBP
145 million to 65.5 million YBP
199.6 million to 145.5 million YBP
251 million– 199 million YBP
299 million– 251 million YBP
359 million– 299 million YBP
416 million– 359.2 million YBP
443.7 million– 416 million YBP
488.3 million– 443.7 million YBP
542 million– 488.3 million YBP
4500 million– 542 million YBP
Cool
Warm
Cool
Warm
Cool
Warm
Cool
Warm
Cool
Warm
Cool
79°F (25°C)
63°F (17°C)
50°F (10°C)
Average Global Temperature
© Infobase Publishing

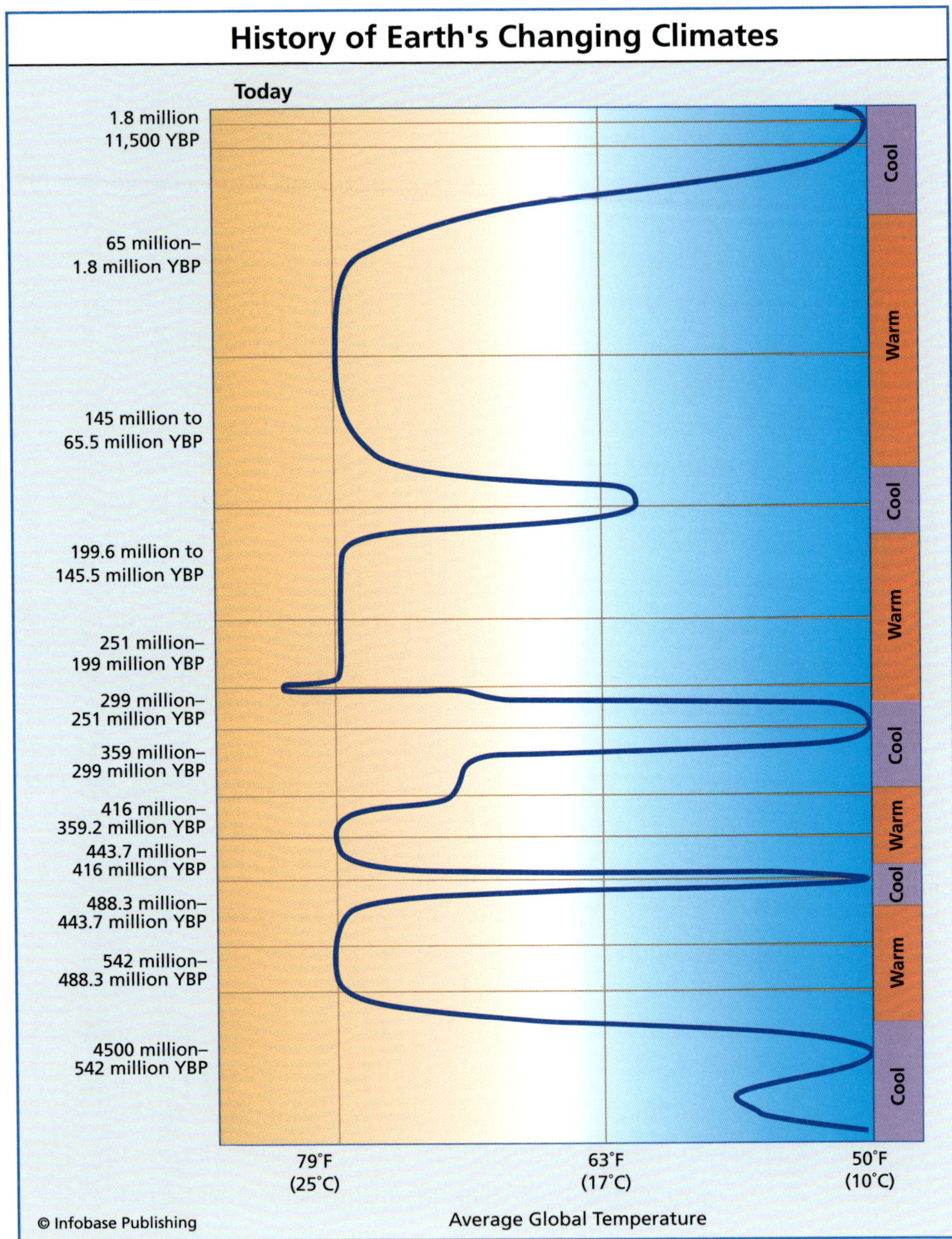

Figure 1

Our planet has also sweltered through four lengthy periods of hot house temperatures. One hundred million years ago, for example, average temperatures near the equator were several degrees warmer than they are today. Polar regions were also much warmer than at present. Worldwide, temperatures, on average, were about 18°F (10°C) higher than today. Interestingly, this condition—a warming of the polar regions—parallels the current pattern of global heating. Very little temperature change is occurring in tropical or middle latitudes. Most of today's global warming trend is affecting temperatures in the polar latitudes.

While these very early temperature shifts are of interest to many scientists, they had no direct impact on humankind. For all practical purposes, humans and the Pleistocene (Ice Age) go hand in hand historically. Both began around two million years ago. About 11,500 YBP, the Pleistocene gave way to the Holocene, a warming geologic epoch that continues today. During the Pleistocene, scientists have determined that alpine (mountain) and continental (ice sheets) glaciers advanced and retreated up to twenty times. There were four major periods of glacial advance. They were separated by interglacial periods during which temperatures warmed. Today, the planet is experiencing a fourth interglacial period. Mother Nature has not revealed whether she intends to grasp the planet in yet another of her icy clutches. If the past offers a clue to the future, however, another frigid glacial advance may well be what the planet's future holds in store.

RECENT CLIMATE CHANGES

To speak of events of the past 14,000 years as "recent" may seem strange. But in geologic terms, this span of time represents about one second on a 24-hour clock. The current epoch of geologic history is called the Holocene. It represents a time during which post–Ice Age temperatures began to rise and ice started to melt. But the Holocene has had its roller coaster–like ups and downs.

The "Big Freeze"

Close on the heels of the end of the Ice Age, Earth's temperatures plummeted again. The period from about 12,800 YBP to around 11,500 YBP is known as the Younger Dryas, or the "Big Freeze." In Europe, temperatures plunged to levels 12° to 16° (7°to 9°C) colder than today. The Americas also suffered. It was during this period that many large animals became extinct. In the New World, horses and camels, mammoths, saber-toothed tigers, and mastodons were among the megafauna that vanished. Some scientists blame the extinctions on a colder climate. They believe the animals died out because they could not adapt to the cold and to the changes in their natural habitat caused by lower temperatures.

A Rapid Warming

About 11,500 YBP, temperatures again began to rise very rapidly in some places. In central Greenland, evidence locked within the island's glacial ice indicates that temperatures rose by about 15° (9°C) *within a single decade*! This event is very important for several reasons. First, it is a whopping temperature increase within a very short period of time. Second, the rise in temperature far exceeds even the most extreme estimates of temperature increase during the twenty-first century. Third, this sharp increase resulted from natural, not human-influenced, conditions. Fourth, it is significant that the greatest warming occurred in the Arctic, the region in which most of today's temperature increase is occurring. Finally, if this large a temperature change occurred over the span of a single decade today, much of the world would be thrown into sweltering chaos. It would be extremely difficult if not impossible for cultural systems to adapt to that great a change over such a short time.

The warm trend continued. During a 4,000-year span that lasted from about 9,000 to 5,000 YBP, temperatures also were several degrees warmer than they are today. During this period, called the Holocene Climate Optimum, it was the polar regions that experienced the greatest warming. By 2000 B.C., temperatures once again began to drop and glaciers began to spread down mountain slopes and across portions of the far northern latitudes. Temperatures would remain relatively cool for nearly three millennia.

Medieval Warm Period

More reliable data have allowed paleoclimatologists to do a better job of measuring recent climate changes. They know, for example, that from about A.D. 800 to 1300, Europe (and certainly other areas of the world) experienced a period of warming. During this time, called the Medieval Climate Optimum or Medieval Warm Period, temperatures were about 4° (2.5°C) warmer than today. But balmy temperatures were not to last long. Nature is fickle, particularly when it comes to climate.

The Little Ice Age and Its Consequences

Between about 1400 and 1850, much of the Northern Hemisphere was plunged into a period so cold that it came to be known as the Little Ice Age (LIA). Average temperatures in Europe and Northern America (the United States and Canada) dropped by as much as 8°F (5°C). In northwestern Europe frigid temperatures caused massive crop failures that resulted in widespread famine and death. In Finland, perhaps a third of the population died from starvation or disease.

Throughout the affected area, farming patterns changed. Only the hardiest of crops could survive the short, cool growing season. Viticulture (raising grapes) disappeared entirely from most of northern Europe. The impact of this change is clearly evident even today in European drinking practices. Before the onset of the Little Ice Age, grapes thrived throughout nearly the entire continent. But during the LIA, they disappeared from the northern areas. Today, throughout southern Europe, vineyards dominate many landscapes and wine is the beverage of choice.

A CHILL COMES TO WESTERN EUROPE

From about 1400 to 1850, much of the Northern Hemisphere was locked in the frigid grip of the Little Ice Age. Temperatures were much colder than today, and snowfall was much greater. Snow fell in places where it had never been seen. Alpine glaciers advanced, destroying farms and villages nestled in mountain valleys. Throughout Western Europe, rivers, canals, and lakes froze over for months at a time, an event that has not happened since. In England, the River Thames froze over repeatedly. In recognition of the natural event, Londoners held an annual Frost Fair, the first of which was in 1607 and the last in 1814.

In the Netherlands, canals froze over, much to the joy of ice-skaters. Harsh conditions have been immortalized in many paintings of the time.

In northern Europe, beer is the most popular beverage. Its chief ingredient is malted barley, a hardy grain that thrives in the region's cooler climate.

Severe conditions were not limited to northern Europe. Snow storms were much more frequent in Portugal and Spain than they are today. In 1622, the southern section of the Bosporus, the strait that separates Europe and Asia in Turkey, froze over. Snow was reported on mountain peaks in several North African countries at levels not seen in more than a century. Even remote Timbuktu, an isolated trading city on the Niger River at the edge of the Sahara Desert, was flooded at least 13 times. Rather than snow, the colder temperatures increased precipitation in this portion of West Africa. As far away as China, some warm weather crops disappeared from places where they had grown for centuries.

To the west, across the North Atlantic Ocean, conditions were also much colder during the Little Ice Age. In Iceland, crops failed. Sea ice surrounded the island for miles in every direction. This made navigation impossible, as well as fishing, upon which Icelanders depend for much of their food supply. These combined events resulted in widespread starvation and a sharp drop in the island's population. By the early 1400s, harsh times had reached Greenland and its small Norse colony. Crops began to fail, including hay and other forage for livestock. With dwindling food supplies, the Norse colonies eventually vanished. The last actual evidence of a living Norse presence in Greenland is a church record dated 1408.

The chill of the Little Ice Age even reached North America. There are many accounts of both Native Americans and European settlers suffering from the severe cold. During the early 1600s, ice remained on Lake Superior until early June. By comparison, severe cold during the winter of 2008–2009 caused the greatest freeze-over of Lake Superior in three decades. Nonetheless, shipping resumed in late March. In 1780, New York Harbor froze over. Residents were able to walk across the Hudson and East rivers and between Manhattan and Staten islands.

Twentieth-Century Conditions

During the twentieth century, temperatures once again increased about 1.3°F (0.75°C). Such a gain is not at all unusual. It has happened on many previous occasions. The Intergovernmental Panel on Climate Change (IPCC) reported that the period between 1995 and 2006 included 11 of the hottest 12 years recorded since 1850. Other sources, however, suggest that the current rise in temperature peaked in 1998 and that temperatures have actually dropped since that time.

According to the four agencies that track Earth's temperatures, something amazing occurred in 2007. The global temperature plummeted by 1.26°F (0.7°C), the fastest drop since temperatures began to be recorded. In 2008, the global temperature averaged 57.76°F (14.31°C), the coldest in nearly three decades. And during the winter of 2007–2008, the Northern Hemisphere had the deepest snow cover since 1966. During 2009 many locations also experienced record cold temperatures. If the cooling trend since 2000 continues at its recent pace, the planet will be 1.3°F (0.72°C) cooler by the end of the century.

HOW RELIABLE ARE THE DATA?

Some scientists question the reliability of recent temperature data that point to global warming. A recent study by Anthony Watts, "Is the U.S. Surface Temperature Record Reliable?," contained some rather shocking information. Watts conducted a national survey of official weather recording stations. He found that 89 percent—nearly 9 of every 10 such facilities—failed to meet National Weather Service standards for station location. In other words, the thermometers were located in places where they were subjected to "artificial" heating. Such sources include dark asphalt roads and parking lots, air-conditioning exhaust fans, hot rooftops, and near walls that radiate heat. Additionally, many official weather stations are located at airports. Many such facilities are now surrounded by urban sprawl where temperatures are affected by the urban heat island. (Temperatures in a large city can be many degrees hotter than those in the surrounding countryside.)

In regard to worldwide changes in climate, scientists now realize that they do not necessarily occur everywhere. One part of the world can warm while another area cools. This pattern continues today, as the locations experiencing temperature extremes can and do shift frequently. During recent years, some areas have sweltered in record heat, while others shivered in record cold. It must be remembered that official weather stations are not evenly distributed. Large areas such as the Sahara Desert or Siberia may be underrepresented in terms of data.

What is happening? Is Earth heating or cooling? Is it possible that natural forces, rather than "hot air" from politicians and others, really determine climatic trends? In the following chapter, you will learn about those forces that are responsible for changing climates.

3

CAUSES OF CLIMATE CHANGE

Weather and climate change constantly. Nighttime temperatures, for example, are usually cooler than daytime temperatures. This daily temperature cycle is caused by the simplest of all Earth-sun relationships. The sun is the source of insolation (**in**coming **sol**ar radi**ation**). This radiant energy is the engine that runs changes within Earth's atmosphere. Simply stated, when the sun is shining in a particular location, the planet receives its energy. When it sets, energy (heat) is lost to the atmosphere. Throughout the day, the sun's position changes relative to any location on Earth's surface. This change is caused by Earth's rotation (spin) on its axis. Atmospheric conditions can also change the amount of energy received and the amount that is lost.

Seasons come and go. In the middle and higher latitudes they bring significant changes in temperature. And in many places seasons bring a change in the amount and type of moisture received. Summer, for example, is usually the warmest and wettest season. With few exceptions, summer moisture falls in the form of rain or possibly hail. Winter, on the other hand, is a season of colder temperatures and less precipitation. In many parts of the United States and Canada, winter moisture falls in the form of freezing rain or snow. Seasonal changes are caused by Earth's revolution—its annual trip around the sun. Rather than being straight "up and down," the planet is tilted about 23.5° from its axis (an imaginary rod that extends through each pole). As a result, when one hemisphere is bathed in more direct sunlight (summer), the opposite hemisphere receives insolation at a low angle (winter).

You may have heard someone, perhaps your parents or grandparents, comment on the "*real* weather" that occurred in the past. They reminisce about a time when temperatures were colder (or hotter). There was more (or less) precipitation. Snow was deeper (or rarely fell). Perhaps ice was thicker (or never appeared). And, of course, storms were meaner (or milder). Many factors influence climates and climate change. Some involve complex interactions between Earth's various spheres: the hydrosphere (water features), lithosphere (land), biosphere (plants and animals), and atmosphere (air). A change in any of the four spheres can cause a change in weather, hence, in climate.

In terms of changing climates, other factors are also involved. Scientists are becoming increasingly aware that the "solar constant" is anything but constant. It was long believed that the amount of energy radiated by the sun (hence, received here on Earth) never changed. Now scientists know that it does change. Rather than always being tilted (relative to Earth's plane of the ecliptic) precisely 23.5°, Earth's axis wobbles. Axial wobbling changes the amount of insolation received at various latitudes. Finally, even Earth's annual orbital journey around the sun changes through time. In this chapter, you will learn how these conditions contribute to changing climates.

Today some people believe that human activity is also causing a perilous change in weather and climate. They worry about various greenhouse gases that humans are adding to the atmosphere. There is concern that these gases may be contributing to global warming. There are, of course, other (often strange)

HOW THE SOLAR ENERGY SYSTEM WORKS

Charts with lots of arrows and numbers can be quite confusing. But if you follow this one closely, you will learn how Earth's atmospheric system works in terms of heating. There are several things you need to know to understand how the atmosphere heats and cools:

1 Earth receives incoming solar radiation (short-wave energy) at the outer atmosphere. The amount (100 percent) was long believed to be a "solar constant." Today, atmospheric scientists recognize that there are slight periodic differences in the amount of energy received and how it is distributed about Earth's surface.

2 As the solar energy penetrates the atmosphere, about 20 percent of it is reflected back into space by clouds and another 6 percent is lost from reflection by the atmosphere itself. Once it strikes Earth's surface, another 4 percent is lost from reflection back into space. Another 19 percent is absorbed by the atmosphere or clouds. About 51 percent actually reaches Earth's surface and is converted to long-wave energy, or heat. Many other factors can also cause these amounts to vary from time to time.

3 Finally, during the short term, at least, Earth's average temperature remains fairly constant. But as you already have learned, over the long run, temperatures can change drastically—from ice age conditions to conditions much warmer than today. Under normal conditions, 100 percent of the incoming solar radiation and resulting heat is lost back into the atmosphere. If, however, the atmosphere's ability to retard the radiation back into space—as with the

suggestions to explain recent warming. For example, one head-line claims "Scientist Implicates Worms in Global Warming." Another cites a study claiming "Obesity Contributes to Global

greenhouse effect—then conditions can warm. If, on the other hand, conditions such as cloud cover or atmospheric water vapor change, temperatures can also change.

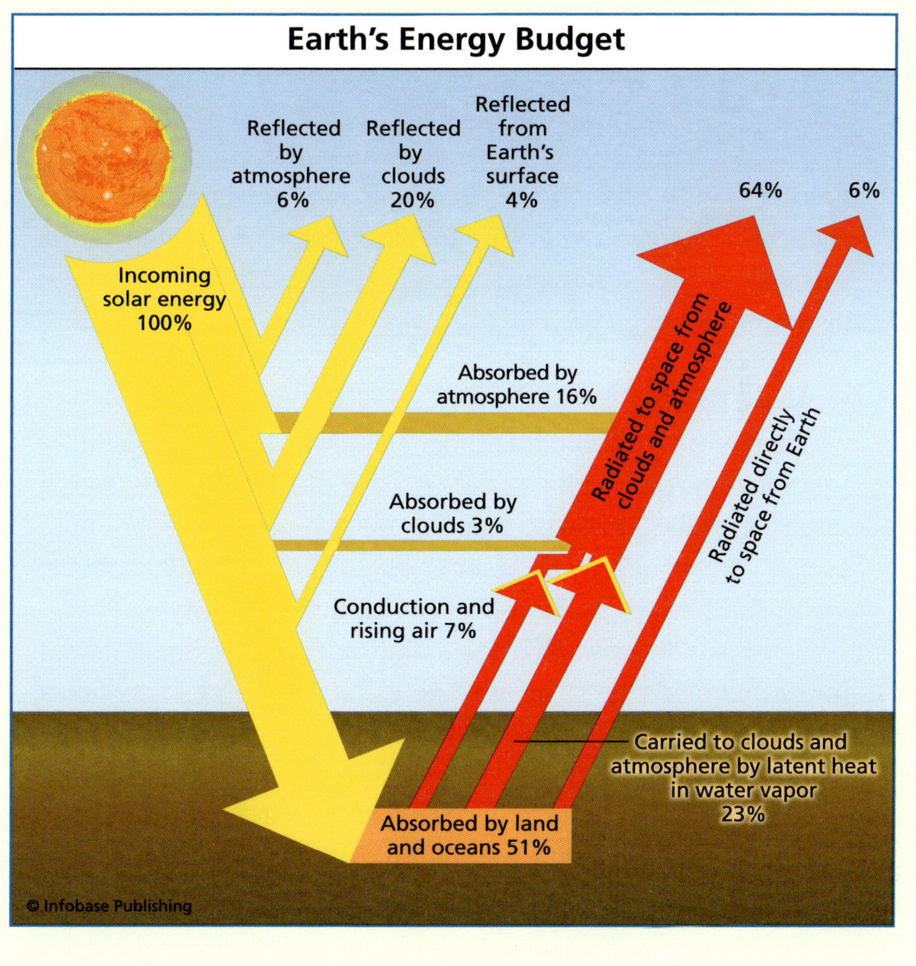

Warming." Do you *really* want to help stop global warming? Then perhaps we all should heed the advice of this headline from an Australian source: "Eco-Friendly Kangaroo [slang for flatulence] Could Help Global Warming: Scientists." What won't some scientists think of next!

CHANGES IN INCOMING SOLAR RADIATION

Earth receives only a tiny portion of the sun's radiant energy. Imagine a very bright, unshielded bulb suspended high over your head that casts light in every direction. Now take a grain of sand and hold it about a city block away from the light. How much of the bulb's light strikes the pebble? A similar amount of solar radiation is received on Earth's surface. Yet this miniscule amount of insolation is our planet's primary source of energy. It provides light and is the engine that drives all of Earth's weather conditions. All life ultimately is dependent upon solar energy. In the context of this book, attention is limited to the ways in which differences in insolation influence weather, hence, climate.

Solar Energy Output

As mentioned above, scientists long believed that the amount of solar energy received on Earth's surface did not change. During recent decades, however, satellite measurements of the sun's energy output suggest that it does vary slightly from time to time. These changes appear to be linked to sunspot activity.

Scientists have known for some time that sunspots occur in a cycle of about 11 years. The difference in the amount of energy emitted by the sun between extremes of sunspot activity seems small, about 0.1 percent. Even this tiny difference, however, is believed to influence Earth's temperatures. When sunspot activity is at a maximum, warmer weather usually occurs. When there are few sunspots, temperatures tend to be cooler.

The 11-year sunspot cycle is not always as reliable as clockwork. Sunspot activity, for example, was minimal from 1645 to 1715, a period called the Maunder minimum. During the 70-year span, temperatures were also much colder than normal. Since minimal sunspot activity and a long period of cool temperatures coincided, some scientists believe they were related. They theorize that the decline in sunspot activity resulted in decreased insolation during the Maunder minimum. This, in turn, was responsible for the cooler weather. Recent developments suggest that this may be true. Sunspot activity in 2008 and 2009 was at a minimum not seen since the Maunder minimum. The global temperature during these years also experienced a marked decline, with 2008 being the coldest year in three decades.

Orbital Changes

The amount of insolation received also varies due to changes in Earth's orbital revolution around the sun. Much of what is known about the relationship between orbital changes and climate was first suggested by a Serbian scientist, Milutin Milanković (1879–1958). (In English, his name often appears as Milankovitch.) In what is now called the Milankovitch theory (See Figure 2), he proposed some startling new ideas. Based upon years of observations and research, he suggested that changes in Earth's movements relative to the sun were responsible for changes in climate. Of particular interest, Milankovitch believed that orbital changes were responsible for the cycles of glacial expansion and contraction during the past million or so years.

In simple terms, Milankovitch proposed that three variations of Earth's orbit influenced climatic conditions: precession, obliquity, and eccentricity. Combined, they influence solar forcing. This is the amount of insolation received on July 1 at 65° North latitude. At first, few scientists agreed with his ideas. By the 1970s, however, it became possible to take core samples of deep-ocean sediments. Based upon these findings and others, many scientists began to accept Milankovitch's theories.

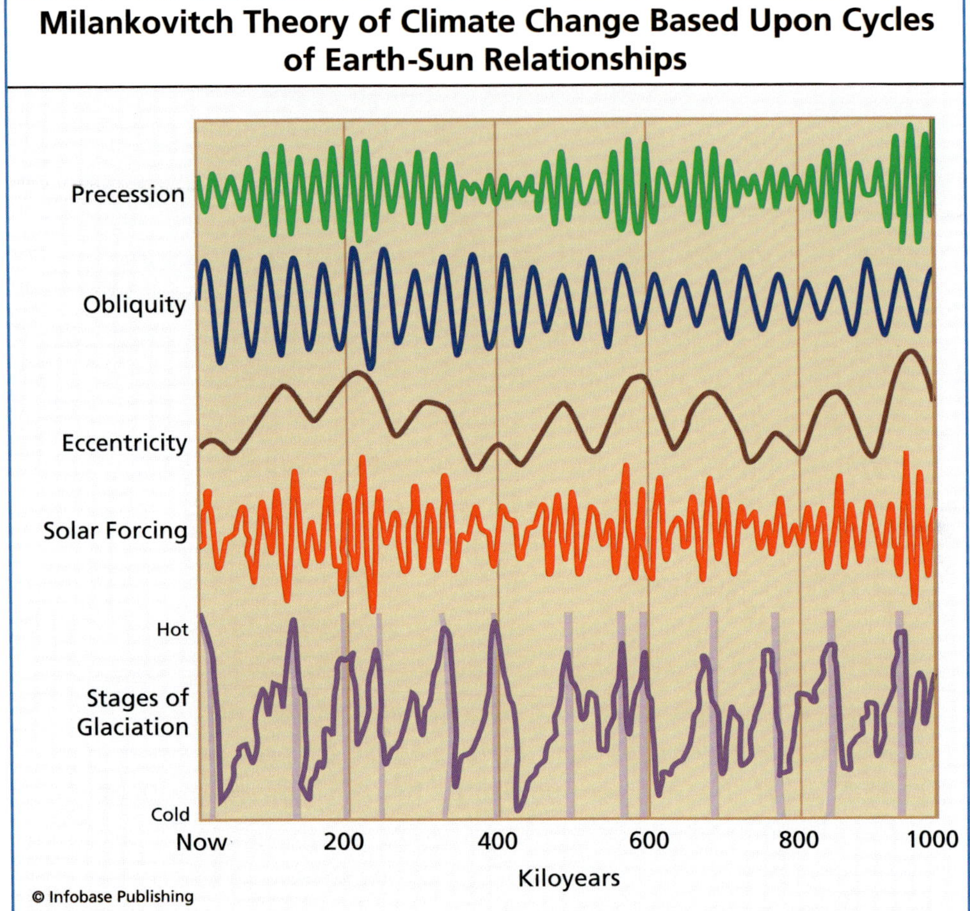

Figure 2

The first cycle is precession (See Figure 3). It results from the wobble of Earth's axis of rotation relative to the North Star (and other fixed stars) and follows a cycle of about 26,000 years.

To best understand precession, think of a spinning top. Most tops have a small piece that extends outward from the upper center. As the top spins, this extension begins to wobble. This is exactly what happens to Earth's axis. Because of the wobble, different portions of Earth's surface receive more (or less) incoming solar radiation from time to time. The Northern Hemisphere has more land (land heats faster and to a greater extreme than water) than does the Southern Hemisphere. Therefore, when precession favors insolation received in the Northern Hemisphere, Earth's temperature warms slightly.

Obliquity, or the angle of Earth's axial tilt, is responsible for the second cycle (See Figure 4). On average, Earth's rotational axis is tilted about 23.5° from the plain of the ecliptic. But this angle changes from 22.1° to 24.5° over a cycle of about 41,000 years. Today, the angle of tilt is 23.44° and decreasing. When

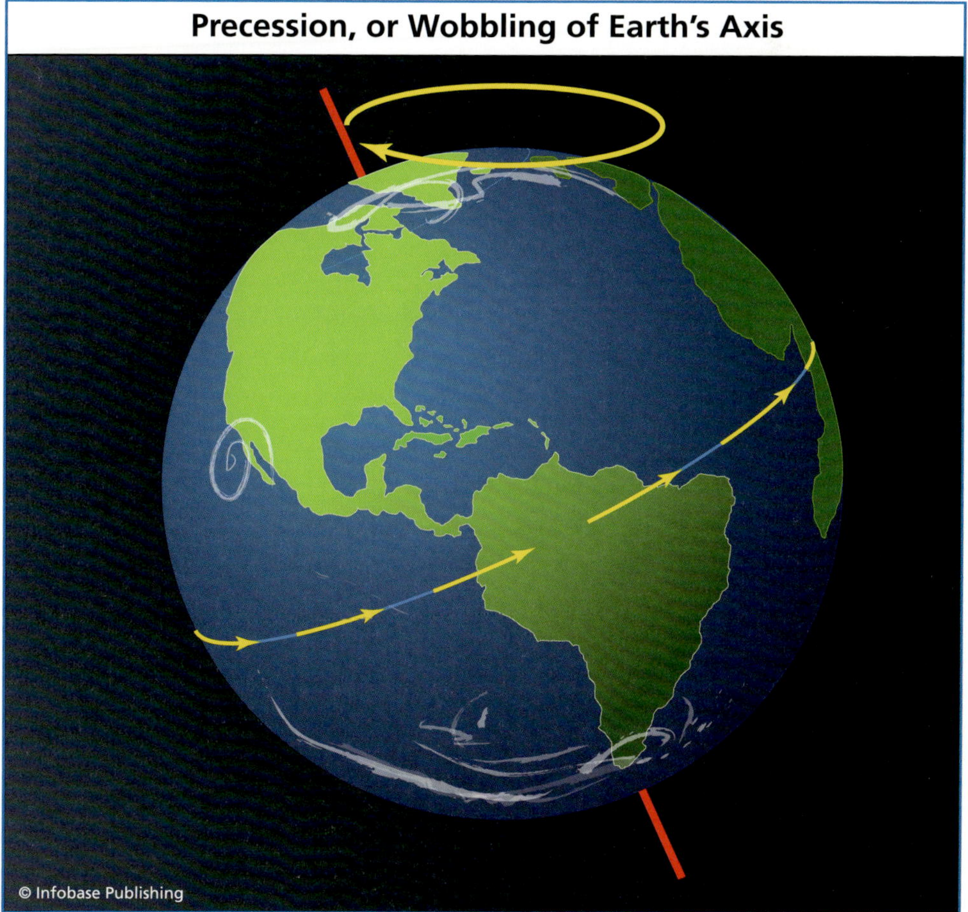

Figure 3

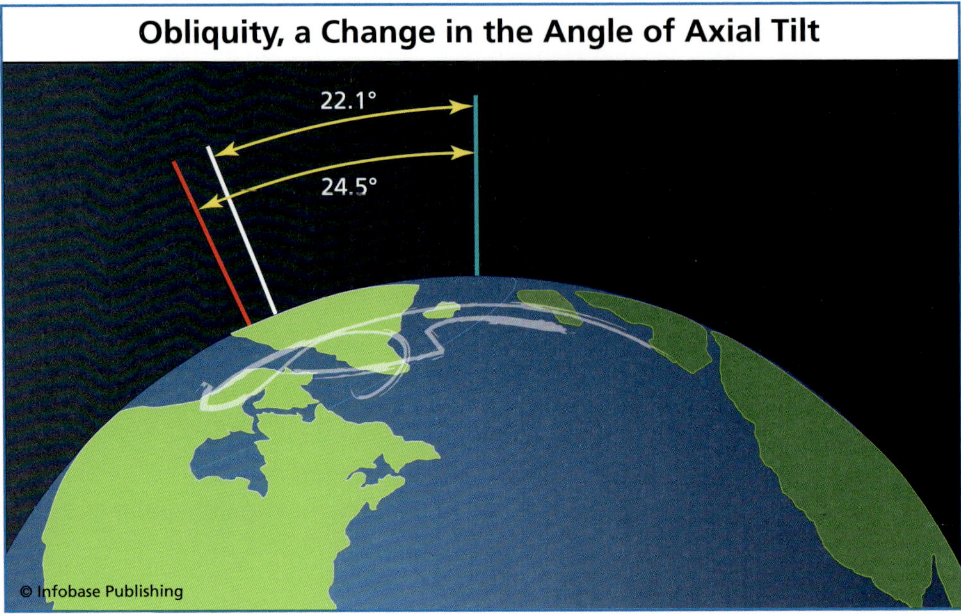

Figure 4

obliquity decreases, as it is doing today, winters tend to become warmer and summers somewhat cooler than average.

Finally, there is eccentricity. It is a measure of the distance Earth is from the sun during its elliptical orbit, or revolution (the planet's 365¼-day annual passage around the sun). The orbit is not a circle. Rather, it is elliptical in shape, being sometimes closer to the sun and sometimes farther away. In January, Earth reaches perihelion ("near the sun"), a distance of about 91 million miles (147 million km). In July, the planet reaches aphelion ("away from the sun"), a distance of about 95 million miles (152 million km). This difference in distance amounts to about 4 million miles (6.4 million km). It accounts for a change of about 6.8 percent in solar radiation received by our planet. Earth's orbit, by the way, is not the cause of seasons. The Northern Hemisphere winter occurs when Earth is closest to the sun, and summer occurs when it is farthest away. Eccentricity follows a cycle of about 100,000 years, which closely matches periods of ice age glacial expansion and contraction.

What does this all mean? You have seen that Earth's movements relative to the sun contribute to cycles of about 26,000 years, 41,000 years, and 100,000 years. Of course, Earth can be in the low of one cycle, the high of another, and midway in a third. As you can see, forecasting long-term changes in Earth's weather and climate can be a very confusing task. This situation helps to explain one scientific study done several decades ago. It claimed that long-term cooling began 6,000 years ago and will continue for another 23,000 years. Yet another recent study suggests that the planet's current relatively warm condition will last another 50,000 years. Which forecast is right? No one really knows.

CHANGES IN EARTH'S SURFACE

Changes in Earth's surface can have a major long-term impact on weather and climate. Two of the most important conditions are the distribution of land and water surfaces, and terrain.

Land-Water Distribution

In order to understand the importance of land and water surfaces, you need to know how each warms and cools. The basic principle is that a land surface will heat and cool faster and to greater extremes than will a body of water. Perhaps you have experienced this principle yourself. Have you ever noticed that if you go swimming during the daytime water feels colder than the air, but at night it seems much warmer? This is because the temperature of the water stays pretty much the same, while the air temperature changes. During the day air is warmer than the water and at night it is somewhat cooler.

Several conditions combine to create the temperature differences between land and water. Basically, they are explained by the different rates of heating caused by continentality (land) and marine (water) influence. First, it takes nearly five times as much solar energy to heat water than it does soil or rock. Therefore, a solid surface will heat much faster than will water. Second, sunlight (radiant energy) can penetrate water, but not land. As a result, land heats rapidly at the surface and becomes quite hot. (Have you ever felt how much cooler soil is a few inches below the surface?) Third, when the sun sets, land quickly gives up its surface heat to the atmosphere. Water, on the other hand, is heated to a considerable depth. As a result, it gives up that heat very slowly because it is spread over a much greater area (in this case, depth).

You can easily see this principle at work. In the summer, millions of people flock to the beach. Why? One major reason is that a coastal location is probably cooler and more comfortable than land far inland. On the other hand, during winter months, the coastal area will be warmer. Those of you who live in an area with cold winters certainly have seen this principle at work. In the fall or winter when temperatures begin to drop below freezing, the land may freeze, but a lake will still be clear of ice. In the spring, however, a lake may remain frozen over long after land conditions warm up. You can also use the Internet, newspapers, or other sources to check temperatures of coastal cities and compare them with those of interior locations. Almost always, interior locations will be warmer in summer and cooler in winter than will coastal areas.

Drifting Continents

Have you heard of plate tectonics? This is the idea that Earth's outer shell is made up of huge plates that slide over a subsurface of molten material. (This is why so many earthquakes and volcanic activity take place along the edge of tectonic plates.) About 225 million years ago, today's land masses fit together much like a gigantic jigsaw puzzle. There was one huge supercontinent called Pangaea. Gradually, about 180 million years ago, this supercontinent began to break apart. (Visuals showing this geologic continental drift through time can be seen on numerous Web sites. Simply search "plate tectonics.") What, you may now be wondering, do "floating continents" have to do with changing climates?

Plate tectonics caused climate change in two significant ways. First, Pangaea was a huge landmass. It would have warmed and cooled to great extremes (the principle of continentality). But as the landmasses spread apart and became surrounded by ocean water, temperature conditions would have moderated somewhat. A second way drifting landmasses experienced climate change really had little to do with climate itself. Depending upon where you live, imagine the following situation. During the winter, you travel 1,000 miles (1,600 km) north and the same distance south. Would you expect temperatures to be colder northward and warmer southward? Of course! You moved, but the climate did not change. As huge chunks of Earth's surface slid about over the planet's surface, they changed latitudinal locations. Antarctica, for example, has fossil remains of life that existed only in much warmer climates than the continent experiences today. That is possible because Antarctica drifted from a mid-latitude location to its present location in the South Polar region.

Landforms and Climate

Land features, particularly mountains, have a major impact on weather and climate. Again, in order to understand this effect, you must think in a geologic time frame. Many of Earth's mountain ranges are quite young. In the western United States, the Sierra Nevada (about 4 million years) and Cascade Range (about 7 million years) are mere youngsters as far as mountains go. By comparison, the Appalachians are nearly 500 million years old. In most mid-latitude locations, wind blows from the west most of the time. As it blows over an open body of water, it tends to take on the temperature of the water over which it crosses.

California, for example, is bordered by a cold offshore current. As a result, coastal cities such as San Diego, Los Angeles, and San Francisco are somewhat cooler during the summer than are inland locations. Mountains, however, block the flow of cool air into the interior. A distance of only about 250 miles (390 km) separates San Francisco and Death Valley. But air moving eastward from the coast is blocked by the lofty peaks of the Sierra Nevada. Coastal San Francisco experiences an annual average temperature of 58°F (14°C), with hot/cold extremes of 103°F (39.4°C) and 39°F (4°C). Inland, Death Valley experiences a much warmer 77°F (25°C) annual temperature average and has recorded a sizzling high of 134°F (56.7°C) and a low of 15°F (-10°C). Clearly, the presence of a mountain range has had a major impact on the weather and climate of those lands lying to the east of the Sierra Nevada.

Winds also give up most of their moisture on the windward (wind-facing) side of a mountain barrier. As they descend down

MAKING C◍NNECTI◍NS

VOLCANOES AND CHANGING CLIMATES

Scientists have found mounting evidence that violent volcanic eruptions can cause sharp changes in the planet's weather and climate. The greatest changes are those caused by what are called super eruptions. These violent blasts are very rare, but when they occur they are thousands of times more powerful than any eruption in recent memory.

The island country of Indonesia has experienced some of history's most violent volcanic eruptions. On the island of Sumatra, several massive explosions are believed to have occurred 840,000, 700,000, and 75,000 years ago. As you would expect, scientists know more about the most recent eruption. They believe the volcano exploded with a force perhaps 3,000 times greater than the 1980 blast of Washington's Mount Saint Helens. So much rock debris and other pollutants were blown into the atmosphere that the average global temperature may have dropped by 5 to 9°F (3 to 5°C), triggering a brief return to ice age conditions. Recently, scientists examining evidence the leeward (away from the wind) slope, they experience a "rain shadow," or drying condition. Again, using the western United States as an example, a precipitation map shows moist conditions on the western flank of the Sierra Nevada and Cascades. On the rain shadow eastern side, however, conditions are much drier. This is the desert region of the Great Basin. A number of locations west of the mountains receive more than 100 inches (250 centimeters) of precipitation annually. Much of the Great Basin, on the other hand, receives less than 10 inches (25 cm) of moisture each year. Most of bone-dry Death Valley gets less than 2 inches (50 millimeters) of precipitation annually. As you can see,

from ice cores and seashells have come to a startling conclusion. The eruption may have caused deep ocean temperatures to have dropped by as much as 10°F (5 to 6°C). As temperatures plummeted, many species could not adapt and became extinct. Some scientists believe that even humans were almost driven to extinction.

During recent centuries, other volcanic eruptions have had a short-term impact on global weather. In 1815, Indonesia's Mount Tambora erupted in what was the most violent such event in recorded history. The two years following the eruption were the coldest (worldwide) in two centuries. In what is called "the year without a summer," crops failed in North America and Europe, causing widespread famine. More recently, global temperatures dropped up to 1°F (0.6°C) following the eruptions of Mount Pinatubo in the Philippines and Mexico's El Chichón.

As you can see, events that occur even in a distant place can have a huge impact on weather throughout much of the world. In this way, all of the planet's locations are much more closely interconnected than many people realize. How might the next "big blow" in Indonesia or elsewhere impact weather and other conditions where you live?

when these mountain ranges formed, they greatly changed the climate of lands lying both to the west and east. A similar situation exists with the Himalayas, the immense mountain range in South Asia. These mountains began to form about 50 million years ago. The tectonic plate that became India slammed into the southern part of the continent. Working like a bulldozer, the crashing plate eventually pushed the Himalayas to elevations that tower above those of any other range. In fact, more than 100 of its peaks rise above 23,600 feet (7,200 meters). They form a huge wall that blocks the moisture-bearing monsoon winds that seasonally blow northward off the Indian Ocean. Much of interior Central Asia is a parched desert landscape as a result. And it has been this way since the Himalayas formed.

CHANGES WITHIN THE ATMOSPHERE

Changes in the makeup of the atmosphere also have an impact on climate. This, in fact, is what the global warming issue is all about. Some people, including many respected scientists, believe that humans are changing the climate. They are particularly concerned about the anthropogenic (caused by humans) addition of carbon dioxide (CO_2) to the atmosphere. (This topic is discussed at length in chapters 5 and 6.) Carbon dioxide, water vapor, methane, and other atmospheric gases combine to create a "greenhouse effect." This term comes from the effect created by the glass roof over most greenhouses.

Short-wave solar energy passes through a greenhouse roof built of glass. But the long-wave energy (heat) created by the insolation can't pass back through the glass into the atmosphere. It is trapped within the greenhouse. The greenhouse effect, in essence, can be thought of as being an atmospheric "blanket." It makes temperature conditions warmer on Earth's surface by trapping heat within the atmosphere's lower altitudes. As the proportion of gases within the atmosphere changes, some scientists argue, so can weather and climate.

Of the various greenhouse gases, far and away the most important is water vapor. A change in the amount of atmospheric moisture can drastically affect climate. Were moisture not present in the atmosphere, Earth's temperatures would be much warmer in the daytime and much colder in the nighttime than they are now. In fact, the planet would be uninhabitable for humans.

During the period extending from the 1940s to the late 1970s, average temperatures dropped. It cooled so much, in fact, that many "experts" feared that the planet was on the brink of another ice age. Some scientists believed that man-made pollution also played an important role in the cooling trend. They thought that man-made pollution helped form more clouds. Increased cloud cover, they reasoned, blocked incoming solar radiation, thereby causing a drop in temperatures. Isn't it strange that some scientists believe atmospheric pollution causes a drop in temperatures while others believe pollution causes temperatures to rise?

CLOSING THOUGHTS

As you think about the information presented in this chapter, there are several things you should keep in mind. First, it is important to remember that throughout Earth's history, climates have changed repeatedly. Second, temperatures at various times have been much colder or much warmer than they are now. Finally, weather and climate are the result of a combination of very complex environmental factors, some of which remain poorly understood by scientists. (Many climatologists and others believe that we may only have scratched the surface when it comes to knowing how the atmosphere works.) Next, you will learn about yet another important aspect of climate—how it affects other elements of the environment, including humans and their activities.

IMPACTS OF CHANGING CLIMATES

A change in climate triggers changes in a great number of other things. At one time, much of the planet experienced conditions much warmer than today. Certainly many things within the natural environment were much different then. And obviously conditions were vastly different during the millions of years large portions of Earth's surface were buried beneath glacial ice. Many people believe that we now face a major crisis because of warming temperatures. Should temperatures continue to rise many changes will occur—some bad, others good. Unfortunately, most news we hear about global warming is negative. Everything seems to point to a "gloom-and-doom" scenario if temperatures increase. It is unfortunate (and rather dishonest) that we rarely read or hear anything positive about a warming climate.

In this chapter, the approach to climate change is presented in the context of the big picture. Emphasis is on the major environmental changes that occur when conditions become warmer or colder. Attention is also given to very general patterns of human adaptation to such changes.

THINGS WORKING TOGETHER

In order to understand how climate affects many, if not most, of the environmental elements, you need to think in terms of systems. Basically, a system is a combination of closely related parts that function as an interrelated whole. No doubt you have heard references to many of them. For example, we have an economic system, a political system, and a social system. You may attend a school system, and your home is probably connected to electrical, water, and sewage systems. When you travel, you may follow the Interstate Highway System. Whether in the natural world or in the realm of human activities, we are surrounded by hundreds of different systems. Each of them is unified in some way by things that work together by making connections.

In regard to climate, the systems concept is best illustrated by weather conditions. Each climate has its own characteristic conditions. They include temperature, precipitation, atmospheric pressure, wind, and storms. In this context, however, we are most concerned with the ways in which different climates impact other environmental elements. This is the concept of ecosystems. (Ecology is the interrelationship between living organisms and their environment.)

Think of three ecosystems: a desert, a tropical rain forest, and the one in which you live. If you live in a desert region of the western United States, you will have to think of someplace else, perhaps along the Pacific Coast.) Now, think of five ways in which each of these environments is different from the others. Now, consider where on Earth's surface you would go to find each of the ecosystems. If you need help, you can get an atlas and sneak a peak at the climate map. Can you identify spatial relationships, such as the wet tropics and tropical rain forests being located near the equator?

Don't put the atlas away just yet. Does it have maps that show the locations of various physical features? You would want to look at maps of climate, precipitation, natural vegetation, soils, and perhaps major types of land use (such as farming, ranching, and so forth). Do you see any relationships between and among the various natural elements? What about land use practices? If you are able to identify relationships between, say, climate, vegetation, and land use, you have taken a huge step in learning about systems—how things work together. The rest of this chapter looks at the ways in which climate affects other geographical elements.

CLIMATE AND LANDFORMS

Geomorphologists (scientists who study landforms) often speak of land features in the context of the climates in which they form. For example, they study "desert" landforms, "tropical" land features, and "Arctic" terrain. Each climate zone has its own combination of temperature, precipitation, surface moisture, wind, and other elements that create distinctive land features. Space does not allow a detailed explanation of how each element works to shape the land, so here we'll just touch upon some high points.

Landforms are created by two fundamental and opposing forces. Tectonic forces are forces that build landforms. They include faulting, folding, and volcanic activity. Climate has no direct effect on these forces. The second set of forces includes those that tear landforms down and deposit their rocky debris elsewhere. These agents include weathering, mass wasting, and erosion. And as you will see, weather and climate play an important role in each of these processes. Let's consider each of them individually.

Weathering is the breaking up of rock material into smaller pieces or chemically taking it into solution. As the name suggests, weather (hence, climate) is a major factor in weathering.

Those who live in areas of Northern America that experience repeated subfreezing temperatures during the winter may have heard the following bit of folk wisdom: "[The state or province in which you live] has two seasons: winter and road repair!" Why road repair? When temperatures rise above freezing, moisture seeps into cracks in the highway. When the water freezes, it exerts a huge amount of pressure—almost 30,000 pounds (13,000 kilograms) per square inch! Continued over a period of time, this pressure causes a breakup of the cement.

The same process can be seen at the base of mountains in areas where repeated freezing and thawing occurs. A talus slope, a huge accumulation of rock debris, forms on the mountain flank. Scree (the rocky material) weathers away from the mountain face and accumulates at the base. In hotter lands, simple day-to-night heating and cooling can cause the gradual disintegration of rocks. Moisture also takes some types of rock into solution. This, for example, is how most caves and sinkholes are formed in areas with soluble limestone rock.

Mass wasting is the process of down–slope movement of earthen material of any size due to gravity. Examples include slow creep, slow to rapid flows and slides, and rapid falls. This process can be accelerated by land becoming saturated with moisture, which adds weight to the earth material. Moisture also reduces friction over a solid surface, thereby making slippage easier. Most if not all areas of Canada and the United States that have sloping land experience mass wasting in some form. Can you find examples in the area in which you live?

Erosion is the transportation of weathered rock material. It is accomplished by moving water, continental and mountain glaciers, and the wind. Some streams transport a tremendous amount of silt. It is often said, for example, that Louisiana is a gift of the Mississippi River. Silt eroded from various places in the river's drainage basin has been deposited to create much of the land that is now Louisiana. Strangely, the work of moving water is most evident in desert landscapes. The reason is that in a desert environment, scant moisture contributes to very sparse vegetation. In the absence of thick plant cover, water runs off very rapidly after a storm.

Glaciers also sculpt the land. Much of the spectacular terrain in the western United States and Canada was scoured by mountain glaciers. Elsewhere, huge continental glaciers, or ice

Erosion created by alpine glaciers millions of years ago sculpted the canyons and valleys of Grand Teton National Park in Wyoming.

sheets, scoured the trenches now occupied by thousands of lakes. They also removed earth material from one area and deposited it elsewhere—often thousands of miles away. In the United States the Pleistocene (Ice Age) glaciers reached southward as far as the present-day Ohio and Missouri rivers.

Finally, wind also creates a small number of landform features, the best known being sand dunes. Although there have been many references to the formation of natural bridges by wind erosion, this is not the case. Nearly all of them are formed by stream erosion.

As you can imagine, when climates change, the importance of the various agents of weathering and erosion also change. Simply stated, those agents at work shaping the landforms of Northern America today are vastly different from those at work during the Ice Age.

CLIMATE, PLANTS, AND ANIMALS

You might recall that in Chapter 2, three of the biotic clues that scientists use to determine climate change are fossil remains of plants and animals, tree rings, and pollen. This works because a very close relationship exists between climates and their associated flora (plant life) and fauna (animal life). This relationship is so strong, in fact, that some climate classification systems are based upon the type of vegetation a climate supports. Perhaps you have seen terms such as tropical rain forest, savanna, desert, mid-latitude grassland, taiga, or tundra used in reference to climatic zones. Yet each of these names identifies the dominant vegetation within an ecosystem, not the climate itself. Nonetheless, because climate is so important to plant cover and animal habitat, it is very easy to associate one with the other.

The relationship between climate and vegetation (whether natural or cultivated) is one of the easiest to understand. All plants have an environment within which they can survive. Limits are imposed by conditions such as temperature, growing season, and moisture. If it is warm and moist, plants of many types will grow in profusion. If it is cold or dry, most plants will be unable to survive. This is why some experts suggest that more than 80 percent of all terrestrial (land surface) organisms inhabit the tropics. Doesn't this suggest that if temperatures warm, Earth can support a greater, rather than reduced, variety and abundance of flora and fauna? It is when conditions become cooler and drier that plants and animals begin to drop out. They simply cannot survive the harsher conditions.

Animal life is adapted to many environmental conditions, the most important (for most fauna) being temperature, water availability, and vegetation cover. Some fauna, such as most of Africa's wonderful variety of large animals, survive in grasslands. So do

MAKING CONNECTIONS

CLIMATE, SEA LEVEL CHANGE, AND MIGRATION

Horses and camels originated in the Americas. Why, then, are we taught that Spaniards introduced them to the New World? And why are camels common to arid parts of Asia and North Africa but found here only in zoos? The answer, of course, is that they migrated. From their initial homeland in the Americas, horses and camels gradually moved northward. According to one theory, these and other species were able to cross the Bering Strait land bridge (Beringia) and enter Asia. They then became extinct in the Americas.

If you reread the last few sentences of the preceding paragraph, you might see climate change at work. "They gradually moved northward" suggests warming conditions that allowed them to expand their habitat into northern latitudes. "Cross the Bering Strait land bridge" to Asia . . . wait a minute: There is no bridge linking North America and Asia! Well, at least not today. Hold tight; we'll return to this topic

Northern America's animals such as prairie dogs, antelope, and grassland bison (there were also woodland bison in the United States and Canada). Others are adapted to woodland conditions. These include squirrels, bears, and many birds. Some animals, such as deer and rabbits, are at home in either environment. When climates change, changes also occur in temperature, moisture availability, and vegetation cover. In other words, a changing climate also changes the habitats to which species of flora and fauna are adapted.

Scientists have long wondered why there are periods in Earth's history during which massive extinctions occurred. Dinosaurs roamed Earth for about 160 million years but vanished about

in just a minute. And then there is the passage, "They then became extinct in the Americas." You already learned that climate change is one of the leading theories to explain the extinction of the New World megafauna.

Now we'll get back to the "land bridge" idea. During the Ice Age, a huge amount of seawater was locked up on land in the form of glacial ice. As a result, sea level was about 400 feet (120 m) lower than it is today. Does the wall map in your classroom show shallow sea water in a light blue color? If it does, most of the light area would have been dry land during the Ice Age. Can you find islands or continents that at one time were linked by land? One such place was Beringia—today's Bering Strait—which was dry land until about 11,000 years ago. Many scientists believe that the land bridge was also the route taken by early humans who migrated from Asia into the Americas.

Can you find other places where early humans might have migrated across dry lands that are now seafloor? In this way, climate change opened migration routes that connected many places.

65 million years ago. Some experts believe that their extinction was caused by a sharp change in the global climate, possibly caused by a huge meteor strike. Much more recently, at the end of the Ice Age about 11,000 to 12,000 years ago, many of the New World megafauna (huge animals) became extinct. They include the woolly mammoth, mastodon, saber-toothed tiger, short faced bear, giant sloth, camel, and horse. Several theories have been advanced to explain their disappearance. Perhaps the most reasonable hypothesis is that they disappeared because of the rapid habitat changes brought about by the end of the Ice Age. Perhaps these and other animals simply were unable to adapt to the rapidly changing environmental conditions. Not only did temperature and precipitation change, but so did the vegetation upon which many depended for their survival.

CLIMATE AND SOIL

Soils are formed by a combination of natural conditions. They include parent material (the earthen material from which the soil is formed), climate, vegetation, microorganisms, slope, and time. Parent material, in some locations, is the result of water, glacial, or aeolian (wind) deposition, each of which is climate related. Slope can be altered by weather-related mass wasting, weathering, and erosion. Temperature and moisture also influence soil formation. Most soils contain organic material called humus. It is broken-down organic matter such as decomposed roots, parts of plants, or even worms and other microorganisms. And here, again, you must think in terms of habitat. Climate determines the environments in which various types of organic life, including microorganisms, can survive. Climate and vegetation, as you have seen, are very closely related. A very close relationship exists between soils and the ecosystems in which they form.

Climate also influences soil erosion. During the 1930s, "Dust Bowl" conditions occurred throughout an area that extended from north Texas into Canada's Prairie Provinces. Severe drought and high winds resulted in the loss of many feet of topsoil in some places. Millions of acres of cropland were destroyed, and hundreds of thousands of people were forced from the land.

Stream runoff from rain or snow melt is responsible for eroding soil from millions of acres worldwide. What is eroded in one place, of course, is deposited elsewhere. Many of the world's most fertile soils are alluvial (water deposited) in origin. They are found in river floodplains, on coastal plains, and in basins.

CLIMATE AND WATER FEATURES

The relationship between climate and water is obvious. At the simplest level, there are wet places and dry places based upon precipitation. Where moisture is abundant, many streams form through which water eventually flows back to the sea. In those places where water is scant, such as a desert, landscapes are parched. Temperatures determine whether water exists in liquid or solid form. Currently, the world's glaciers—both ice sheets and those in high mountains—appear to be in retreat. As the ice melts and runoff enters the ocean, sea level rises. And you have already learned that about 90 percent of the world's natural lakes were formed by glacial erosion.

CLIMATE AND FOSSIL FUELS

Fossil fuels—coal, petroleum, and natural gas—were formed up to 300 million years ago. As their name suggests, these energy sources are the fossil remains of organisms. They were created by the decomposition of phytoplankton and zooplankton (tiny plants and animals that live in the sea). And for them to have lived in such huge numbers suggests that climatic conditions had to be favorable for their growth.

Today, the fossilized remains of these minute organisms provide most of the energy needed to power our economy. In 2006, the Energy Information Administration estimated that 86 percent of all energy used worldwide comes from fossil fuels. The breakdown is petroleum (36.8 percent), coal (26.6 percent), and natural gas (22.9 percent). Unfortunately, the burning of fossil fuels is a primary source of carbon dioxide, the greenhouse

EARLY HUMANS AND CHANGING CLIMATES

Throughout much of human history, people were limited in terms of where they could live. Our original homeland was the warm, moist, tropical environment of equatorial East Africa. Biologically, we are tropical "animals." Perhaps a million years passed before humans possessed those cultural traits that made possible their eventual migration to colder lands. Nothing was more important than control of fire. It provided warmth and protection against fierce animals, and greatly added to the food humans could digest. Other things were needed, such as protective clothing, a means by which water could be stored and carried, and adequate shelters. Once they possessed these things, early humans began a journey that ultimately would take them throughout much of the world.

Not only have humans survived many major changes in the global climate, we have also moved freely from one climatic zone to others. An excellent example of humankind's ability to adapt to changing climates is the migration that brought the earliest people to the Americas. Traditional wisdom points to a migration across the Bering Strait land bridge (Beringia). But here we find ourselves embroiled in one of the greatest mysteries that confronts social scientists: What some archaeologists believe to be the oldest evidence of an early human presence in the Americas is not in Alaska, where it should be if humans came via this route. Rather, it is in the southernmost part of South America! Let's leave it to others to solve this mystery. Our concern here is with changing climates and human migration.

gas that is believed to be the primary contributor to global warming. Yet we are extremely dependent upon fossil fuels to support not only our own, but the entire global economy. How many ways can you think of in which you would be affected if 86 percent of your energy supply was sharply reduced? You can

Let's suppose that these early migrants did travel across the frigid Arctic environment of northeast Asia and northwestern North America. Somehow they survived in a landscape dominated by glacial ice and spots of barren tundra vegetation. From there, they moved southward into the vast taiga forest. Here, game was plentiful, but winters were severely cold. Gradually, they entered the more temperate middle latitudes. Here, summers were warm and winters were somewhat milder than those to the north. Soon, however, a new and much more challenging environment confronted them—the desert, with its scarcity of water and vegetation. Somehow, though, they made it through.

By the time they reached present-day Central America, they entered a seasonal wet-and-dry climate and rugged mountainous landscapes. Farther south they reached one of the world's greatest barriers, the towering Andes Mountains. If they traveled to the west of the mountains, along the Pacific coast, they would have experienced the world's driest place, the bone-dry Peruvian-Atacama Desert. If they chose to venture east of the Andes, they would have been in the vast humid tropics and dense tropical rain forest of the Amazon Basin. Migrating still farther southward, they would have entered one or more mid-latitude climatic zones and related ecosystems. Finally, they settled down in the bitter cold area of southern Chile. And according to the dates associated with various archaeological sites in the Americas, the journey was made in just a few thousand years. Now *that* is an amazing record of human achievement in the face of changing climates.

The Eggborough Power Station, a coal-fired plant near Selby, United Kingdom, is pictured above. The burning of fossil fuels is a primary source of carbon dioxide, the greenhouse gas that is believed to be the primary contributor to global warming.

see the dilemma that decision makers face in knowing which way to turn in regard to energy production and use.

HUMANS AND CLIMATE CHANGE

Weather and climate play a very important role in almost everything that humans do. This relationship—human ecology—is studied by scientists in many fields including anthropology, cultural geography, agriculture, and others. Human ecologists, regardless of their scientific background, study ways humans interact with the environment. Basically, they want to know how people adapt to, use, and change the environment in which they live.

Humans have been around for several million years. Obviously, our ancestors were confronted by and survived many changes in climate. Sometimes conditions were much warmer than today and at other times much colder. With each change, however, they managed to adapt to the new conditions. Surprisingly, perhaps, it appears as though they were able to make the necessary changes with little trouble.

If people are able to make a living (by whatever means) in a particular environment, they will settle there regardless of its climate and other environmental conditions. The major exceptions are very high mountains and polar ice caps. Yet even in Antarctica, there are temporary populations of scientists, and the Greenland ice sheet has both scientists and military personnel. When oil was discovered in Alaska, the state's population soared. During the past half century, bone-dry Arizona and Nevada have been the two fastest-growing states in the United States. And for the last half century, the desert cities of Phoenix and Las Vegas have been two of the country's most booming urban areas. Some of the world's highest population densities are found in the sweltering, humid, tropical environment. Humans are highly adaptable.

As a population density map reveals, densities tend to be greater in warmer lands than in colder places. This is something to keep in mind as you consider the effects of possible global warming. Think about it: Is life easier and safer where it is extremely cold or where frost seldom if ever occurs? In the following chapter, you will learn about the science of climate change, including possible global warming.

THE SCIENCE OF GLOBAL WARMING

Certainly, you have seen TV or newspaper weather reports that forecast conditions for the coming week. But have you ever followed up to find out if they got it right? If, let's say, on Sunday evening the weather announcer forecasts rain for Thursday, how often does it actually rain that day? Just for fun, why don't you keep a record for, say, a month, just to see how often the forecasts are correct.

This is not to discredit meteorologists. All things considered, they do a wonderful job. Their forecasts are particularly good for severe weather events, a service that has saved countless lives. It is amazing, for example, how they can say with some certainty that "X miles southwest of [community], there is a tornado on the ground. It is traveling at Y miles an hour and will strike [the community] in Z minutes. Residents must seek shelter immediately!"

But it is important to remember that their predictions are based upon state-of-the-art weather information. Meteorologists have access to models based upon historical weather data. They also rely upon computers, Doppler and other radar data, radio-sonde-equipped weather balloons, weather monitoring satellites, and other scientific methods. Yet they often fail to correctly forecast tomorrow's weather, let alone what will happen during the week ahead! With this in mind, how can one be certain that 50 or 100 years from now Earth will be a sizzling wasteland as some people suggest? The answer is very simple, they can't.

Meteorologist Roy Spencer perhaps summed up forecasting best: "The deeper we probe and the more we learn, the less we understand, and so the more amazed we are at how nature works." Spencer went on to suggest that "it could be that science has only scratched the surface when it comes to knowing how the climate system regulates itself." His views reflect those of a great number of respected atmospheric scientists.

GROUND RULES

In this chapter, we will attempt to steer clear of the emotion-charged environmental, political, economic, and social issues related to global warming. These will be addressed in Chapter 7. But before you read the "hype," you need to know what the issues really are. That is, what does science have to say about Earth's recent warming trend? Here, every effort is made to stick to the facts, rather than interpreting them to fit some preestablished "agenda." So, as we proceed, it is extremely important that some ground rules be established to serve as guideposts for the discussion that follows.

1. For the past (roughly) three decades, Earth's temperatures have been warming. This warming, itself, really is not the issue. What is in question is: (a) whether the current warming trend is unusual, (b) does the warming pose a serious threat to humankind and the environment, (c) is the warming natural or

anthropogenic in origin, and (d) is the recent cooling the beginning of a new natural trend or a short-term event?

2. The past century has experienced a substantial increase in carbon dioxide (CO_2) and several other greenhouse gases within the atmosphere. Their primary source is the rapid increase in the use of fossil fuels (coal, petroleum, and natural gas) during the same period.

3. The *possibility* (and some would say a *very strong probability*) exists that the increase in atmospheric greenhouse gases and global warming are related. So far, however, this link remains a *theory*, rather than a proven fact.

4. Finally, it would be foolhardy for humans to ignore negative feedbacks from the natural environment based upon human activities. Positive steps absolutely must be taken to ensure a safe, clean, productive, and sustainable environment for future generations. The question is how, at what cost, upon whom, and with what consequence(s) will such measures be imposed?

WHAT IS GLOBAL WARMING ALL ABOUT?

In 1827, a French mathematician, Jean Fourier, was the first to suggest that certain atmospheric gases act like a greenhouse. Basically, "global warming" is the theory that Earth's temperature is increasing at a rate that cannot be explained by natural causes. By far the leading explanation for this event is the greenhouse effect. It, in turn, is caused by an increase in greenhouse gases believed by many to be anthropogenic in origin. There are a number of greenhouse gases. The most important is water vapor. Were it not for water vapor in the atmosphere, Earth's average temperature would be about 54°F (30°C) colder, or just a few degrees above 0°F (-18°C)! Other important greenhouse gases include carbon dioxide (CO_2) and methane (CH_4). There are several others, such as nitrous oxide (N_2O) and fluorinated gases, but they contribute only a tiny fraction to the total greenhouse effect.

As the global warming/greenhouse effect theory goes, these gases form an atmospheric "blanket" that holds heat close to Earth's surface. On average, about half of the short-wave solar energy reaches Earth's surface. There, it is converted into long-wave energy, or heat. Heat, in turn, radiates back into the atmosphere. (This is the major reason temperatures begin to drop at night after the sun has set.) But greenhouse gases trap some of the long-wave energy (heat) as it rises. The net effect is a warming of Earth's surface and the lower atmosphere.

During the past century, global surface temperatures have increased slightly, about 1.33°F (0.74°C) ± 0.32°F (0.18°C). The

Members of the United Nations Intergovernmental Panel on Climate Change hold a press conference at the close of the IPCC XXVII in 2007. The panel is composed mainly of politicians with various agendas, not of scientists.

United Nations Intergovernmental Panel on Climate Change (IPCC) predicts a further probable rise in temperature of 2.0 to 11.5°F (1.1–6.4°C) during the remainder of the twenty-first century. An increase of that magnitude, in as short a period of time, would, of course, be catastrophic. Based upon the IPCC estimates, we should all rush out and buy as many shares of air-conditioner manufacturers' stock as possible! Much of the IPCC projection is based upon recent increases in atmospheric CO_2. (As you will learn later, most members of the IPCC are not scientists. Rather, they are political appointees who know little if anything about how the atmosphere works.)

If you go online, you can easily find any number of graphs that show a sharp increase in atmospheric CO_2. At first glance, it

MAKING C⊕NNECTI⊕NS

WE'RE ALL IN THIS TOGETHER!

Think for a moment about the ways in which scientific discoveries have benefited your life and that of people throughout the world. We owe scientists a tremendous debt of thanks. Our lives are so much better because of their tireless work.

When you think of a scientist, what comes to mind? Someone who spent years pursuing a graduate degree in preparation for a professional career in a scientific field? Someone who works alone, perhaps for years at a time, in a dingy laboratory? Someone who spends much of his or her life sitting at a computer crunching numbers or attempting to develop a more valid model of the way something works? Someone who spends months, or perhaps even a professional lifetime, trying to identify some new principle or develop some new and useful invention? Someone who after years of tireless work, suddenly runs into a dead end that destroys his or her theory, only to begin again? Someone who because of his or her tireless certainly appears that we have a real problem! But let's crunch some numbers to see what they really mean. The following figures are based upon data from Hawaii's Mauna Loa Observatory. The current concentration of atmospheric CO_2 is about 380 parts per million (ppm). In 1960, the concentration was about 340 ppm. In other words, during the past half century, atmospheric CO_2 has increased by about 40 ppm.

Now, let's look at this in another way. Carbon dioxide amounts to about .038 of the atmosphere. There really isn't very much of it. In fact, at the present rate of increase, human activity adds only about two molecules of CO_2 to every one million molecules of air every year or so. Let's put these figures in terms more easily pictured. Fill a large bucket with water. Now, add *one drop* of

effort has become an authority on one particular topic within one particular science?

Although perhaps a bit stereotypical, this is a fair description of many scientists. The tireless efforts of "reputable" scientists should be respected and applauded. Why is it, then, that today we are willing to place "science" in the hands of so many nonscientists? How much of what you have heard, seen, or read about global warming has actually been learned from scientists? Or are your thoughts on the matter based upon some other source? Perhaps your opinions on global warming are based upon Al Gore's compelling film, *An Inconvenient Truth*, or some other motion picture or TV show. How many Hollywood people are scientists? How many politicians have backgrounds in science, particularly meteorology or climatology? On the basis of what scientific backgrounds do most media people make their "expert" opinions? Whether in regard to global warming, or any other important issue, you must *always* question the background and expertise of the source.

hot water. Would you be able to measure a change in the water's temperature? What about a change in the level of water within the pail? Of course not! A growing number of scientists believe that the CO_2–greenhouse effect theory is just that—a mere drop in the bucket in terms of contributing to climate change.

WHAT IS THE SOURCE OF GREENHOUSE GASES?

Many of the so-called greenhouse gases are products of nature. Humans, for example, really can't do much to change the amount of water vapor in the atmosphere. And water, you will recall, is the number-one greenhouse gas by a wide margin. Most water vapor comes from two sources, evaporation from surfaces and transpiration from plants. Evaporation occurs primarily from the global sea and other surface waters. Transpiration is the process by which plants lose water vapor to the atmosphere. (It is a process similar to animal perspiration.) As Earth heats, evaporation and transpiration increase, thereby increasing cloud cover. Cloud cover, in turn, reduces the amount of insolation that strikes Earth's surface. In other words, some scientists argue that global warming will increase cloud cover which, in turn, will cause the planet to cool.

Carbon dioxide also enters the atmosphere by naturally occurring means. In the context of global warming, however, we are most concerned with the ways humans speed up that process. Plants and animals are sources of carbon. Millions of years ago, there was a time that life on Earth flourished in great abundance. Various organisms died, were buried, and eventually became fossilized. Today we recognize the result of this process as our fossil fuels. When these fuels are burned, whether in homes, vehicles, factories, or elsewhere, their stored carbon is released. Much of it makes its way into the atmosphere.

Methane is another greenhouse gas. It, too, has many natural sources. Most of it is a byproduct of microbes that live in oxygen-poor environments. They include rice paddies and mud in the bottom of ponds. When organic material previously locked in permafrost (permanently frozen ground at high latitudes) is released, it also contributes to atmospheric methane. Animals even contribute methane by passing gas built up in their digestive tracks. During recent decades, rice production and livestock raising have increased. As a result, there has been a corresponding increase in atmospheric levels of methane.

"HOT" AND "COLD" RELATIVE TO WHEN?

Have you been outside today? If so, was the temperature hotter or colder? Very logically, you ask, "Hotter or colder than when, or relative to what?" Temperatures are relative. They are always hotter, colder, or unchanged only in relation to the temperature with which they are being compared. This reality is of extreme importance as we attempt to place today's global warming in perspective. We have all seen references to the current warming that some suggest has reached catastrophic levels. Six hundred million years ago, the planet's *average* temperature was about -58°F (-49°C). This is much colder than the annual average temperature of Antarctica today. Most life, as we know it, could not have lived under such conditions. Doesn't this make you feel somewhat better about today's balmy 59°F (15°C) average global temperature? These warmer conditions support abundant flora and fauna and a population of nearly seven billion people. Ten million years ago, the planet sizzled under an average temperature of 122°F (50°C). How does this compare with today's highest annual average temperature? Dallol, Ethiopia, holds the distinction of being the spot with the highest annual average temperature—a torrid 94°F (34.4°C).

But never mind what happened millions of years ago. That really isn't a fair comparison. Let's consider recent temperatures. We know that our planet was locked in the grip of the Little Ice Age from about 1300 to 1850. Is it fair to compare today's rather pleasant (by comparison) temperatures with those that brought incredible suffering and even death to millions of people? And what about the sharp drop in temperatures that took place between the 1960s and the early 1980s, when many scientists predicted the onset of another ice age? Ironically, some of the same scientists who were leaders in the global cooling scare now support the theory of global warming. As a scientist seeking federal support for one's research, it is always a good idea to be riding the bandwagon that is currently popular!

As you have read elsewhere, our planet has experienced periods during which temperatures were much warmer than those of today. And this has happened repeatedly during Earth's 4.5-billion-year history. As you learned in Chapter 2, current conditions are nothing unusual. To refresh your memory, the graph in Figure 5 shows the concentrations of atmospheric CO_2 and temperature during the past 400,000 years. Do you see anything unusual? The current carbon dioxide level is comparable to those during four previous periods. And temperatures are slightly below the four earlier peaks. Doesn't it appear that atmospheric CO_2 concentrations and global temperature conditions are just about where they should be on the current cycle?

IS THIS HOW SCIENCE WORKS?

Scientists are human. They make mistakes. They also have their own world views, belief systems, and other influences on the way that they think about and approach their research. By now, you certainly are aware that the person writing this information has his own viewpoint. It is one that is quite different from the beliefs most commonly expressed by the media, many politicians, and the Hollywood crowd. It also differs from the views of many scientists. It is, however, an opinion based upon nearly 30 years of research. The "hype" of global warming is the topic of Chapter 7. Here, as promised, the emphasis is on the *science* of global warming.

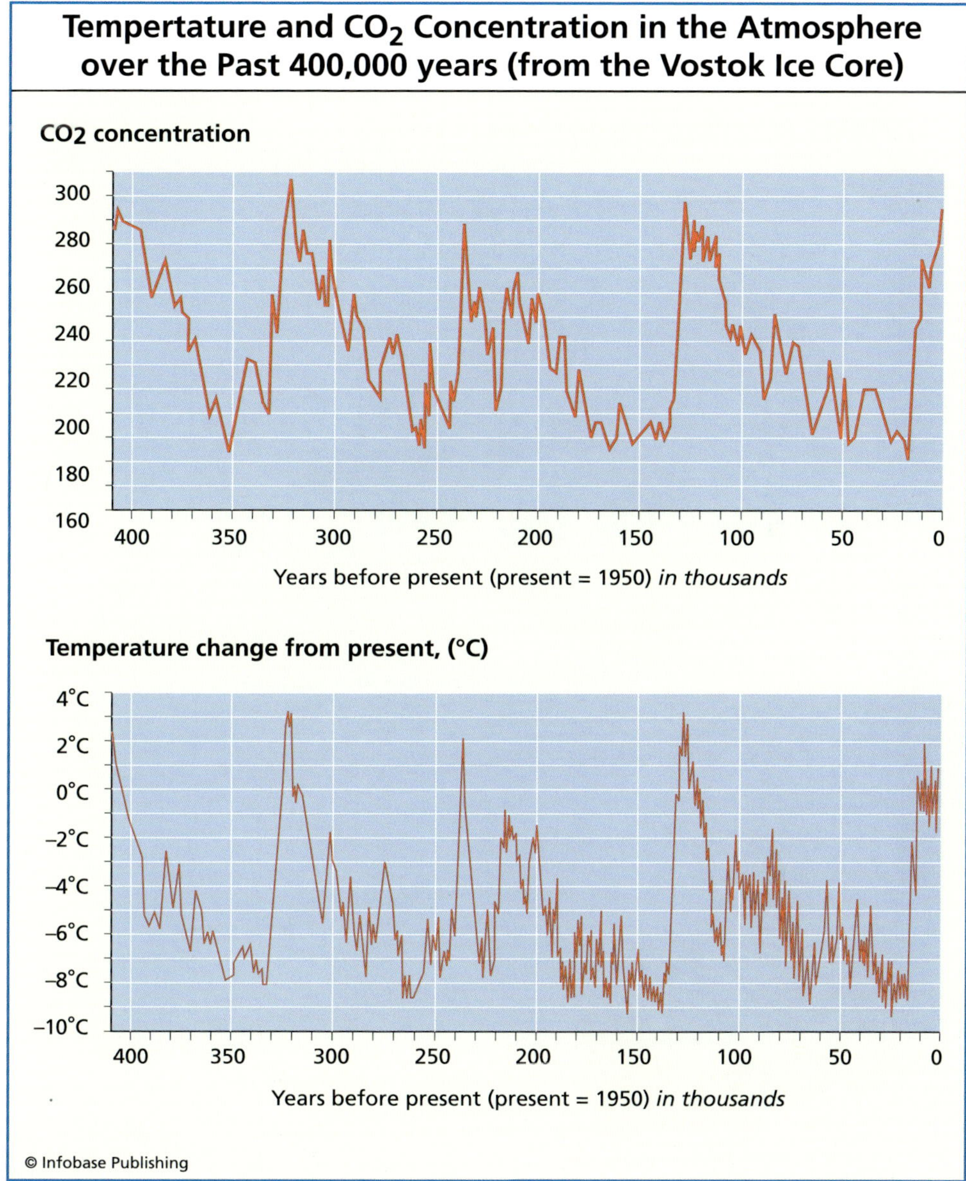

Figure 5

The United Nations' position on global warming is presented by the Intergovernmental Panel on Climate Change (IPCC). This body has boldly stated that "the science is 'settled' on man-made

HOW SOON THEY FORGET!

For nearly three decades, the threat of possible global warming and its consequences has been a major global concern. Yet as recently as the early 1980s, many scientists and others were predicting the onset of another ice age! What is to be learned from the hype first associated with feared catastrophic global cooling and then with that of potentially catastrophic global warming?

global warming . . . the debate over the science of climate change is . . . truly over." This is not the way science works. It is by no means over! As you have seen, it is a scientific puzzle of monumental size and countless pieces, many of which are only now beginning to fall into place.

It is perfectly proper for a scientist to say, "Based on the evidence, I *believe* that (something is, or is not, happening) . . ." It is quite another matter to say, "I *know* . . ." Very few scientific principles, including some "laws," are permanently etched in concrete. Today, even several of Einstein's laws are being challenged by some scientists. About scientific progress, geographer Peter Haggett summed it up by noting that "the sound of progress is the sound of plummeting hypotheses." This conviction was echoed by T.G. Dobzhansky, who believed that "any scientist worth his salt labors to bring about the obsolescence of his own work." Both statements are open-minded, the way scientists should be. Sadly, many advocates of the global warming theory do not follow these important guideposts of scientific research.

It is absolutely essential that science be bias free. If a person with a strong belief is determined to prove or disprove something, he or she almost certainly will be able to do it. Unfortunately a great deal of today's global warming research is of this nature. Have you seen recent scientific studies that suggest global warming *is not* happening? Or even research that strongly supports the theory that it is happening, but due to natural, rather than anthropogenic, causes? Are you aware of any government grants received by scientists who have a theory that opposes the scripted scene of anthropogenic, greenhouse-caused global warming? Have you seen a TV news special, an article in a weekly news magazine, or any other medium that featured possible global *cooling* and its consequences? In each case, probably not! This simply is not the way science works or the way reputable scientists should function. When a trial witness is sworn in, he or she must swear to "tell the truth, the full truth, and nothing but the truth . . ." Shouldn't we expect the same from our government, the media, environmentalists, and some members of the scientific community? When climates change, many other things change, both within the natural environment and the realm of human activity. In the following chapter, we will investigate some of these changes and what they mean to Earth's future and to your own.

THE IMPACTS OF GLOBAL WARMING

An estimated $50 billion has been spent in the United States and Canada—by both government and private industry—on global warming research. Scientists have directed most of their attention toward two major questions. First, they want to know whether global warming is actually happening and, if so, what is its cause. Second, many studies have focused upon the various impacts of rising temperatures. (Strangely, very little research has been funded to study the effects of possible global cooling and its impact.) For nearly three decades hundreds of articles and many books have been published, describing countless things that will result from a warming Earth. And according to the "experts," almost none of them will be positive.

Negative results range from increased blindness from cataracts to a plummeting salmon population off the California coast. Swarms of jellyfish in Scotland are blamed on global warming. One headline boldly suggests that "Warming Could Wipe Out Scotch [whiskey]," one of Scotland's most famous products.

Another warns that "Climate Change Will Collapse Earth's Eco-system." Still another predicts that "Warming Will Wipe Out Billions," leaving only about 10 percent of the planet's population alive. What's a person to believe? Is our planet really on the brink of a catastrophic meltdown? Should we fear for our very lives?

There also have been more than a few articles written that predict the onset of another ice age. Were we to believe everything we read, one would be faced with a horrible decision: Would we rather freeze to death or die of heat? This chapter focuses upon some of the more important and realistic consequences of changing climates.

WHAT HAPPENS IF EARTH WARMS?

Let's assume that the planet does continue to warm at a rate forecast by the so-called experts. What will happen? Obviously, many changes will occur. Some, of course, will be bad. But often ignored are the many changes that will be good. As you read the following passages, it will be helpful to keep in mind the "accordion" example from Chapter 2. If Earth does continue to warm, tropical and middle-latitude climates and ecosystems will expand, or move toward higher latitudes. Those of polar latitudes will shrink in size. If planetary temperatures rise, many experts believe that most warming will be in the higher latitudes. Tropical latitudes, in fact, may actually cool a bit. Strangely, in this case, warming would cause cooling. Warming will increase cloud cover. Greater cloud cover, in turn, will reduce the amount of insolation that strikes the surface and becomes heat.

Changing Patterns of Precipitation

Some scientists already see a pattern of precipitation change resulting from global warming. As a general rule, wet places seem to be getting wetter and dry places somewhat drier. Certainly this has happened throughout much of the semiarid and arid United States. Most of the country's western interior, the desert Southwest, and large areas of California have been bone dry during recent years. Water of the Colorado and Rio Grande rivers rarely reaches the sea. Reservoirs such as Lake Mead and

CRYING "WOLF" ONCE TOO OFTEN?

For several decades, experts forewarned of another ice age, a belief widely held by many scientists. Now, several decades later, we are gripped by fear of global warming. Might we be measuring, comparing, and contrasting today's warmer temperatures against those of a cooler recent past?

Over the years, these experts have foreseen many calamities. It seems that humanity is always on the brink of some catastrophe. Perhaps none spread more fear than did the threat of overpopulation that raged during the 1950s and 1960s. One expert predicted that hundreds of millions of people would die of starvation by 1975. Yet since 1960 the population has more than doubled. And today we hear very little about there being too many people. Food production, we were told by authorities, simply could not keep pace with the booming population. Yet today, as a percentage of the human population, far fewer people are hungry than ever before.

Some experts feared that essential natural resources would be gone by the twenty-first century. It didn't happen. In the 1930s some experts cautioned that petroleum would be gone by 1950, if not sooner. Many decades later gasoline still fuels our vehicles and much of our economy. And do you remember the Y2K scare of the late 1990s? Experts had the world's computers crashing at midnight on December 31, 1999. The results, they warned, would be catastrophic.

Have you ever heard the fable about the little boy who cried "Wolf!"? Is there a point at which the public may turn a deaf ear to "experts" and scientific warnings? It would be tragic were that to happen. Science is far too important and complex to be driven by opportunistic politicians, sensationalist media, and a concerned (although generally uninformed) public.

Lake Powell on the Colorado River—the sources of water for millions of people—have been at historic lows during the first decade of the twenty-first century.

Because of its immense population, recent drought conditions have been particularly devastating to semiarid areas of China. Portions of Australia and Africa also have suffered from severe drought conditions that many blame on global warming. Wetter and drier periods, one must remember, also undergo cycles. Recent droughts are nothing unusual. What has happened is that populations have exploded, leaving more people to be affected.

During recent years, the western United States and Canada have experienced an increase in the number of forest fires because of drought conditions. Many fires have been more devastating than normal. Aridity combined with higher temperatures also damages forests in another way. Drought and warmer-than-average winters combine to create favorable conditions for insects such as the mountain pine beetle. This destructive pest has killed millions of acres of coniferous forest throughout much of the western United States and Canada.

Storm Conditions

Some scientists have predicted that warming temperatures will create more and stronger tropical storms (hurricanes, typhoons, and cyclones, depending upon their location). Recent studies, however, seem to discount this possibility. Atlantic hurricane records have been kept since 1881. Between 1971 and 2009 fewer Atlantic hurricanes occurred than during any comparable period for which records exist. This time span also coincides with the recent rise in temperatures.

The greatest number of hurricane deaths, by a wide margin, occurred more than a century ago. Property damage has increased simply because today more people live in hazardous coastal areas. The recent problem with hurricanes (and tropical storms in the Pacific and Indian oceans, as well) is their aim. Temperature cannot "guide" a storm into a major city or heavily

Wildfires ravaged much of California in 2009. With warmer than normal weather in the area, conditions were right for such devastation.

settled coastal zone. Where hurricanes hit is a matter of random luck. And for cities such as Miami, Florida; New Orleans, Louisiana; and Galveston, Texas, their luck finally ran out.

Two other types of storms, both of which take their toll on life and property, would be reduced in number and ferocity in a warming environment—tornadoes and blizzards. Nearly all tornadoes occur in North America. They are extremely rare elsewhere. These often deadly storms are created by a convergence of warm, moist air off the Gulf of Mexico and cold, dry air from Canada. In the absence of frigid Canadian air, they could not develop. Blizzards, too, would be much less frequent and severe if temperatures continued to warm.

Plant and Animal Life

Throughout Earth's history, periods of warmth have been associated with periods of abundant flora and fauna. Even today, perhaps

80 percent of all plant and animal life inhabits the tropical realm. Most organisms thrive in heat; very few are adapted to conditions of severe cold. Despite reports that predict the extinction of many species, from all indications, plants and animals would thrive in a warmer environment. The greatest amount of warming, it appears, is happening in the polar latitudes. There, some species may be unable to adapt to change and may become extinct. Fortunately, the high latitudes are the places that have the fewest species, so a minimal number of organisms would be affected.

It is true that tropical insects would expand their range into what today are temperate lands. Some studies caution that warming conditions will spread malaria, an often deadly disease. Malaria, however, is not limited to the tropics. Outbreaks have occurred throughout the middle latitudes. In fact, the greatest infestation of mosquitoes the author has ever experienced was in Alaska just a few miles from the Arctic Circle! Malaria is a scourge in the tropics simply because of widespread poverty. Poor people are less able to protect themselves against the disease. They cannot afford medication that protects against malaria or insect repellant, to spray mosquito-infested areas, or to enclose living quarters.

Much has been written about plant and animal life that may be unable to adapt to changing climates. Many species, some fear, will become extinct. But you must remember that most animals and plants are mobile. Although they are unable to change their natural habitat, as their habitat either enlarges or contracts in size, they (as a species) can move along with it. The past century has experienced periods of rapid temperature rise and sharp decline. Yet, there is little evidence that such changes contributed to an abnormal loss of plant or animal species. Why, then, is there a widely held belief that so many species are dying out? The answer is simple. First, the human population has doubled during the past five decades. This has caused a loss of natural habitats. Second, when plants and animals move along with their habitat, they can disappear from an area in which they were once common.

There is no better example of this principle than the "disappearance" of Canada's Hudson Bay polar bears. In fact, these majestic creatures have become the poster child for the anthropogenic global warming (AGW) group. Polar bears, they claim,

MAKING CONNECTIONS

WHAT IF EARTH COOLED?

During recent years a growing number of studies suggest that Earth may be entering a cooling period, perhaps even another ice age. In 2004, a headline warned that "Climate Change Will Destroy Us." The accompanying article cautioned that:

Climate change over the next 20 years could result in a global catastrophe costing millions of lives in wars and natural disasters. . . . Nuclear conflict, mega-droughts, famine and widespread rioting will erupt across the world . . . an abrupt climate change could bring the planet to the edge of anarchy as countries develop a nuclear threat to defend and secure dwindling food, water and energy supplies.

Sounds familiar, doesn't it? Well, you might be surprised to learn that the reference was *not* to global warming. Rather, it focused upon the consequences of forthcoming and severe global *cooling.* "Ah . . ." one might say, "That rubbish came from global warming skeptics! What do they know?" Well, are you ready for another shock? The passages were based on a study done for the Pentagon. The report was supposed to be secret but it was leaked to the press. In the United States, it received almost no media attention. (The foregoing passages were taken from a U.K. publication, the *Guardian Review,* 2/24/04.)

After having read this chapter, it might be fun to do a little digging for information. Identify as many positive effects as possible of global cooling. Then list as many negative effects as you can find. After you have made your list, which is longer—good or bad things resulting from cooler temperatures? Which condition—warming or cooling—do you believe would help the greatest number of people worldwide?

are threatened by global warming and, in fact, may even die out. Surprise! Recent surveys have shown that the polar bear population actually has grown during recent years! What's going on? Well, geography can help us answer this riddle.

Although remote, the Canadian town of Churchill is unique because it can be reached by both rail and commercial air service. Until recently, it had a large polar bear population. With easy access and plenty of bears, Churchill became a popular tourist destination. As conditions warmed, however, the polar bears moved northward, away from Churchill. The bear population did not decline. They simply moved to cooler locations some distance from the town where tourists came to see them!

Threat of Rising Sea Level

If all existing ice melted away, sea level would rise about 200 feet (60 m). Some of the rise would come from the meltwater itself. But a considerable amount of the rise would come from thermal expansion (as water warms, it expands). Were this to happen, some estimates suggest that up to half the world's population would be affected. That would, indeed, be catastrophic! Fortunately, not even many AGW pessimists believe this will happen. Most experts, including the Intergovernmental Panel on Climate Change (IPCC), predict a rise of several inches to a maximum of 3 feet (1 m) during this century. Nonetheless, even this rise would be extremely damaging to some coastal areas.

Low-lying coastal plains tend to be very fertile; hence, they attract farmers. In some countries, people flock to coastal areas to live because of their scenery and recreational potential. Many of the world's largest cities are located on coasts, where they grew as seaports. A number of low-lying island countries would be threatened, including the Bahamas.

Of the mainland countries that face a severe threat from a rising sea level, none is in greater jeopardy than Bangladesh. Most of the small South Asian country was formed by silt deposits from the Ganges (Ganga) and Brahmaputra rivers. Bangladesh is so low in elevation that during severe (and frequent) flooding, more than half of its land area is under water. Most of the country's nearly 160 million people live very near sea level. Even a slight rise in the sea would submerge the land on which they now live and upon which they depend for their living. (Bangladesh is about the size of the state of Georgia. But its population is more than half that of the United States and nearly five times greater than that of Canada.)

In the United States, many coastal areas would be threatened, even by a slight rise in sea level. Nearly all cities and other coastal settlements along the entire Gulf of Mexico would be in serious jeopardy. This is particularly true of New Orleans, much of which already lies below sea level. So would low-lying areas along the Atlantic coast of Florida, Georgia, the Carolinas, and Virginia. New York and Boston are among the northeastern cities that would be affected by a rising sea. Given time to adapt, however, measures can be taken to protect cities and lands. (Sixty-five percent of the Netherlands lies at elevations below sea level.)

Sea Ice

Much has been written about the melting of Arctic sea ice. However, because it is already in the sea, melting sea ice does not cause sea level to rise. Is the melting of sea ice really a bad thing? It is, of course, another indicator used by some scientists and others to "prove" that global warming is occurring. On the highly positive side, were the Arctic Ocean opened to shipping, thousands of miles of travel would be saved. Vessels could pass through the Arctic between Europe and Asia without going through the Panama Canal or around the southern tip of South America. This would greatly reduce the amount of fossil fuel burned by ships. Shipping costs, hence, the price of shipped goods, would drop—a benefit to hundreds of millions of people. According to the Arctic Research Center at the University of Illinois, Arctic ice cover is no longer disappearing. In the winter of 2008–2009, the expanse of global sea ice (which includes the Arctic and elsewhere) was equal to that of three decades ago.

Agricultural Production

A number of studies suggest that global warming will severely reduce agricultural production. Catastrophic food shortages, they fear, will occur as the population continues to grow. After all, according to most estimates, there will be around 9 billion people, 2 billion more than the present population, by 2050. How will they be fed?

Do rising temperatures really pose a serious threat to agricultural production? Well, the answer is yes and no. It depends upon what question is asked. Can the world feed itself? Absolutely! There is enough (highly nutritious) kelp off the coast of Southern California to adequately feed the entire world's population. (But would you want to eat kelp every meal for the rest of your life?) Many of the issues that relate to agriculture have little if anything to do with changing climates. So let's limit ourselves to the possible impact of a warming Earth.

It should be obvious that most crops grow better under warm conditions. Factors such as the length of growing season are extremely important to farmers. For many crops, such as corn, summer nighttime temperatures are important. Additionally, warmer temperatures would greatly increase yields in many lands that are only marginally productive today. This includes the hardy grain and potato belt of northern Europe, Russia, and Canada.

There is, however, one extremely important question mark hovering over the role of global warming and agricultural production: precipitation. The less moisture an area receives, the more prone it is to long periods of drought. And today, much of the world's grain is grown in areas that receive 10 to 25 inches (25 to 60 cm) of moisture annually. During the first decade of the twenty-first century, many of the world's major grain-producing areas have experienced severe droughts that have resulted in a sharp drop in yields. Even with this decline, however, there seems to be an ample supply of grain, sugar cane, soybeans, and other crops. After all, a substantial portion of these crops is now used in making ethanol, fuel for vehicles rather than food for people or livestock!

Thawing Permafrost

One of the greatest problems associated with rising temperatures is one that is often overlooked in climate-related discussions: permafrost. Where temperatures drop well below freezing for a long period of time, the ground freezes solid. In the upper middle latitudes, as temperatures begin to warm, the frozen ground thaws. In colder northern latitudes the surface thaws, but at a depth the ground remains frozen. It is this permanently frozen ground that scientists call permafrost. It occurs in much of Canada and Alaska and in a broad belt across northern Europe and Siberia.

Under warming conditions, the active (upper) layer of permafrost thaws out to a greater depth. This creates a deeper "spongy" surface that can cause tremendous damage to structures. Roadways and railroads, for example, begin to buckle as they sink into the mire. Buildings, if not protected, also begin to sink. Protecting against melting permafrost was a huge problem engineers had to overcome in designing the Trans Alaska Pipeline System.

Several methods are used to protect against permafrost. Buildings can be constructed on pilings that extend deeply into the permanently frozen ground and thereby offer support. Another method is to remove the upper active layer of earth and replace it with rock or gravel that will neither freeze nor thaw. This method is used frequently with roads and railroads. Finally, in some instances, the ground is kept frozen artificially during the summer months. All of these methods are extremely costly. If warming continues, some estimates place the cost of protecting against permafrost at trillions of dollars.

Some scientists have asked a very interesting question: Is permafrost melting because of global warming, or is melting

This buckled house illustrates the damage that thawing permafrost can create.

permafrost the chief cause of rising temperatures? As permafrost thaws, greenhouse gases stored within the formerly frozen ground are released. The amount of carbon that is now trapped in permafrost is much more abundant than first thought. In fact, according to some estimates there may be 30 to 100 times more carbon released into the air from melting permafrost than by the burning of fossil fuels! As permafrost thaws, methane, another greenhouse gas, is also released in increasing amounts. Regardless of the cause, if the recent warming trend continues, released CO_2 and methane could cause a rapid acceleration of global warming.

An Ice Age Triggered by Warming?

Confused? Some scientists believe that further warming could start another ice age, at least in Europe. Today, Western Europe is much warmer than its latitudinal position would suggest. This condition results at least in part from the transfer of water heated in the tropical Atlantic. The heat is transported into northern waters by the Gulf Stream and North Atlantic Current. As ice melts from the Greenland ice cap and elsewhere in the Arctic region, a layer of freshwater forms over the North Atlantic. (Freshwater is less dense than saltwater.) As this happens, it is feared that the warm saline current would dip below the freshwater and descend into the ocean depths far to the south of its present location. In the absence of moderating warm ocean water, temperatures throughout much of Europe would plummet.

This chapter has barely scratched the surface in terms of both positive and negative effects of warming temperatures. Hopefully, it has steered you in the direction of searching for additional information on your own. In the following chapter, we will take a closer look at the "hype" of global warming.

THE HYPE SURROUNDING GLOBAL WARMING

Several years ago SARGAS, a Norwegian alternative energy company, had an ad in which a child asks an adult, "What did you do during the war on global warming?" The ad went on to say that the "war on global warming needs more warriors." By now, the reader should realize what the "war on global warming" really needs. Because so much is at stake, it needs more cool heads, less political and media hype, and more serious, non-biased scientific research. In reference to the hot air generated by all the hype, Dr. Vaclav Klaus, president of the Czech Republic, summed up the situation well. He said, "It would be most helpful to the debate on climate change if the current monopoly and one-sidedness of the scientific debate over climate change . . . were eliminated."

For three decades, most discussions of global warming, its cause(s), and its effects have been very one-sided. Fortunately, the tide is beginning to turn. In 2008, for example, there were about 70,000 Web sites devoted to "climate change denial," "global warming hoax," or similar terms. One year later, the number had jumped to nearly 15 million. How often have you seen exaggerated statements to the effect that *"all reputable* scientists believe . . ."? Such statements simply are untrue. First, there are thousands of scientists who do not believe in global warming. Second, such statements claim that scientists who do not support the global warming theory are not reputable. Such statements are inflammatory and have no place in scientific debate.

During recent years, a large and rapidly growing number of reputable scientists have gone on record as *not* believing in anthropogenic global warming. In fact, nearly 31,500 scientists (as of December 2009) have signed the Global Warming Petition Project. The expressed purpose of the project is to:

> . . . demonstrate that the claim of "settled science" and an overwhelming "consensus" . . . is wrong. No such consensus or settled science exists . . . a very large number of scientists [31,478 by late 2009] reject this hypothesis.

> These scientists are instead convinced that the human-caused global warming hypothesis is without scientific validity and that *government action on the basis of this hypothesis would unnecessarily and counterproductively damage both human prosperity and the natural environment of the Earth.* [Emphasis by author]

As a reader of this book, you are obviously concerned about the environment and are interested in the global warming issue. You are to be congratulated! You have shown that you think like a scientist should. You have an open mind and desire to be informed about both sides of an issue in your search for truth.

AN ISSUE FOR MANY AGENDAS

What is at stake in the global warming controversy? By now, you certainly realize that the issue is one about which many people hold strong beliefs. These beliefs, however, vary greatly and many of them have little if anything to do with climate change. It should be left to science—the very best science that scholars can offer—to decide three important questions. First, is Earth's climate actually warming? Second, if the climate is warming, is human activity the cause or is change simply a response to some natural cycle(s)? Finally, what action(s), if any, should be taken in response to possible warming? The problem is that as of now, there are a lot of theories, but not much conclusive evidence. There are lots of nagging questions and a tremendous amount of hype. Of one thing you can be certain: There is a lot of "hot air." The question is whether it is atmospheric or verbal!

All of the hype muddies the water. Very few people are willing (or able) to view the global warming question objectively, taking into consideration both sides of the issue. For many people, anthropogenic global warming (AGW) has become an issue they approach with religious fervor. In Copenhagen, for example, thousands of rioters took to the streets in protest. They accept the "truth" of warming based upon faith and defend their belief emotionally, rather than rationally. It will be very difficult for such people—including an alarming number of scientists—to admit that they may have been wrong if, indeed, this proves to be the case.

Global warming is an issue that fits many agendas. For a small number of scientists, AGW has been a pot of gold. According to some estimates, $50 billion has been spent on global warming research in the United States and Canada alone. Many scientists and others also have linked their reputations and futures to the AGW theory. This helps to explain why global warming skeptics have been so loudly criticized by their peers. One widely respected climatologist and AGW skeptic even

This political cartoon takes a shot at those who believe that global warming is bunk. The issue tends to divide along party lines, with Republicans closing their minds to it and Democrats jumping onboard the global warming bandwagon.

received a number of death threats. Is this the way reputable scientists conduct serious research, threatening with death those who disagree with them?

Anthropogenic global warming is an issue that numerous opportunists can adapt to their own political agendas and worldviews—particularly those related to social change. Unfortunately, when huge sums of money are involved, scientists (among others) do not want to admit that they might be wrong. Let's take a brief look at some of the groups that have adopted AGW to achieve their own goals. Could it be that the hype they generate is the cause of so much confusion? Very few of the people identified below by group association have a background in science. But this matters little to them. Who are some of these "players"? What do they stand to gain from taking a strong stand in support of global warming?

United Nations Intergovernmental Panel on Climate Change (IPCC)

Have you seen references in the media to "over 2,000 scientists representing the Intergovernmental Panel on Climate Change agree [to something related to global warming]"? Actually, the IPCC has very few scientists, particularly those with a background in meteorology or climatology. Since 2002, the panel has been chaired by an economist. Most members are bureaucrats who represent their government and its positions related to global warming. Here, it is important to know that more than 75 percent of the world's countries are poor. As a voting bloc, they can strongly influence decisions made by the United Nations. And it is these countries that stand to benefit—perhaps by trillions of dollars through time—from measures designed to lessen the perceived global warming threat. Of course the IPCC sees a huge threat in global warming. Most less developed member countries will benefit greatly from any decision that transfers wealth from rich to poor nations under the guise of global warming.

The Media

Television, the printed news, and other media have found a cash cow in the global warming controversy. The public, it seems, loves to be scared to death. Fear sells. According to one report, over a four-year span network evening news presented 107 reports of anthropogenic global warming. Not one of them offered a "fair and balanced" assessment by presenting both sides of the controversial issue.

HEADLINES OF CLIMATE CHANGE

The debate is over: Globe is warming
There IS a problem with global warming. . . . It stopped in 1998
Nine of 10 warmest years on record have occurred since 1995
Sun oddly quiet—hints at next "Little Ice Age"?
Climate change will collapse Earth ecosystem
2008 was the year man-made global warming was disproved
Land development eyed as a cause of global warming
Prehistoric man began global warming
Antarctic ice sheet increasing: growth shows global warming
    —Study
Greenland's glaciers have been shrinking for 100 years
Massive Greenland meltdown? Not so fast, say scientists
Melting permafrost scare deflated by new study
Global warming behind record 2005 storms: experts
Expert sees no relationship between global warming and
    hurricanes
Climate change may kill millions in Africa: Report
Genocidal global warming policies will kill hundreds of millions

The following headlines have appeared during recent years. Is it any wonder that so much confusion surrounds the issue of global warming? Who and what is one to believe? Which of these headlines do you believe to be true? On what do you base your beliefs?

Environmentalists ("Greens")

Obviously, everyone should be concerned over environmental quality. But some groups go a bit far. The Voluntary Human Extinction Movement, for example, believes that humans should become extinct. This, they suggest, is the only way our planet can heal. Oil and natural gas fields and coal mining inflict some environmental damage. So, too, does burning these fossil fuels. Pollution is not limited only to atmospheric CO_2. Have you ever experienced smog (smoke and fog), or smust (smoke and dust)? Environmentalists use the fear of greenhouse gas–caused global warming to advance their "green" objectives.

"Cleaning up" the environment, based upon the threat of global warming alone, would cost trillions of dollars. A clean, nonpolluted, safe environment is a luxury that only an affluent society can afford. As studies have shown during the recent economic downturn, contributions to environmental causes have dropped sharply. Many communities have stopped recycling. Some have reduced the number of trash pickups. Environmental restoration projects have been shelved due to the lack of funds. This includes the cleanup of many U.S. Environmental Protection Agency toxic waste sites. When the economy suffers, so does the environment. A major reduction in the use of fossil fuels would devastate the U.S. and global economy. The results would be catastrophic in terms of environmental protection, restoration, and sustainability.

Anti-Americanists

Although America has many friends around the world, there are also many people who are strongly anti-American (including some Americans). The United States is the world's leading user of fossil fuels and second largest contributor of atmospheric CO_2 (behind China). Therefore, the country is a major contributor to anthropogenic greenhouse gases. Additionally, the United States is the only industrial country that has not signed on to the Kyoto Treaty. Many Europeans (among others), in particular, use these two realities to heap blame on the United States.

Has the United States really failed to curb its atmospheric pollution? Hardly! According to data released by the U.S. Department of Energy, between 2007 and 2008 the country decreased its CO_2 emissions by 192 million tons. This was a greater reduction than that of the next leading 35 countries *combined*! The United States continues to use fossil fuels that pollute the atmosphere. But the country is also the world leader in cleaning up its CO_2 emissions. During the same period, China increased its CO_2 emissions by 490 million tons.

Those Holding Liberal Political Views

Former U.S. vice president Al Gore is a Democrat whose strong stand on the AGW issue is highly respected by many people

(continues on page 98)

Former vice president Al Gore promotes *An Inconvenient Truth* in Japan in 2007. Gore was awarded the Nobel Peace Prize that year for his efforts to educate the public about human-influenced climate change. Because of this work, Gore has become a hero to some and a villain to others.

MAKING C⊕NNECTI⊕NS

DON'T EAT CHOCOLATE!

Imagine that scientists found an ingredient of chocolate—let's make up a word, "itroblicate"—that *may* cause illness in rats. Some feared that humans might also become ill if they continued to eat chocolate. Not all scientists, however, agreed. Some pointed to the fact that chocolate has been consumed for centuries. Others argued that itroblicate is present in only very tiny amounts, about .003 percent, or one tiny speck of a candy bar. It didn't take long for the itroblicate question to explode into a major issue involving scientists and countless other interests. Those who continued to eat chocolate or suggested that it was a nonissue began to be scorned and discredited.

The media, knowing that fear sells, immediately began to spread panic. "Itroblicate may kill humans," screamed headlines. Naturally, citizens became deeply concerned. Hardly anyone, however, had the knowledge to judge whether or not itroblicate posed a threat. They depended upon so-called experts (mostly politicians and media people) for their information.

Seeing an opportunity to press their agenda, various special-interest groups jumped on the anti-chocolate bandwagon. Scientists saw a golden opportunity to obtain grant money to further their research. To further study the potential problem, they applied for and received billions of dollars in research funds.

Cacao, from which chocolate is made, is grown on tropical plantations. Environmental groups, concerned over the loss of tropical rain forests, saw the itroblicate issue as a golden opportunity to fight deforestation. Human rights activists joined in the fray. They were concerned that cacao plantation workers in poor tropical lands were not making fair wages. (They seemed to forget that at least the workers had wage-paying jobs.) Animal rights activists, too, were up in arms.

They knew that chocolate is poisonous to dogs. Each group saw the itroblicate scare as an opportunity to further its agenda.

Groups opposed to globalization also jumped on the anti-chocolate bandwagon. The chocolate industry, after all, is a huge business with many global connections. Sugar and cacao are grown on tropical plantations and are processed in many countries into the various chocolate products that we enjoy. Finally, chocolate products are sold in countries, rich and poor, throughout the world. To antiglobalization groups this was not right. Poor people in developing countries were buying (and enjoying) a product manufactured and marketed by large corporations in a developed country. This had to stop!

It didn't take long before politicians became involved in the controversy. They began passing laws right and left that restricted the manufacture and sale of chocolate. The result was that many companies closed. Others, in order to avoid restrictive laws, moved their factories abroad. Either way, tens of thousands of people were left unemployed. Chocolate company stocks plummeted, taking with them billions of dollars in stockholders' revenue.

Many people who believe in socialism saw this as an opportunity to promote a one-world government. They saw the control of chocolate production and distribution as a way to get their foot in the door of global political control. Leaders in many less developed countries recognized that most chocolate is eaten in developed countries. They demanded that they be paid hundreds of billions of dollars, to offset any financial losses that might be suffered by their economies.

In the foregoing example, did you get sidetracked and perhaps forget about itroblicate? Do you suppose any scientists would have received grants to study the possible health *benefits* of itroblicate? How do you think critics or doubters of itroblicate's harmful effects might have been treated by the media and others? Do you see a parallel with the global warming issue?

(continued from page 95)
holding liberal political views. Additionally, from 2000 to 2008, Republicans held the presidency. President George W. Bush and Vice President Dick Cheney both had ties to the oil industry. This made Republicans an easy target for those who support initiatives designed to cut back on the use of fossil fuels.

Many people who hold liberal views believe that global warming will hurt the poor more than the rich. In reality, just the opposite is true. It is the poor who will suffer most from many of the measures designed to reduce greenhouse gas emissions. According to some estimates, several million jobs would be lost in the United States alone, most of them blue-collar jobs. In 2009 Democrats submitted a bill in Congress that calls for an impossible 83 percent reduction in fossil fuel emissions by 2050. Think, for a moment, about the consequences of such a bill and how it would affect you.

If implemented, the reduction would result in much higher costs that, of course, will be passed on to consumers. Home owners and renters, car owners, small business owners, farmers, and many others would pay much more for energy. The cost of essentials like heating, cooling, transportation, food, and other necessities would skyrocket. According to one estimate, if passed, this liberal legislation would cost Americans $9.4 *trillion* by 2035. And much of that burden would fall upon the poor. Paying for essentials, after all, takes a greater percentage of their income than that of the wealthy.

Those Opposed to Big Business

Estimates vary, but certainly the energy business is America's largest. A substantial percentage of the nation's economy depends upon energy. Many people, however, resent large and successful businesses. They believe that many businesses take advantage of consumers and earn unfair profits. The truth is that the United States has a standard of living second to none. And the lifestyles that its citizens enjoy are largely the result of a strong and stable economy. Perhaps the critics of American businesses and the American economy should spend some time in a less developed country. They might gain a greater appreciation of their own nation. Many of the measures designed to "punish" the American energy industry would throw the United States and Canada into a deep financial crisis. The prosperity and benefits that citizens of both countries now enjoy would be lost. Unfortunately, the economies of less developed lands would also be destroyed.

CALAMITY OR SCAM?

John Coleman, founder of the Weather Channel and a respected meteorologist, has called global warming "the greatest scam in history." In a November 2007 news release, he admitted to being "amazed, appalled and highly offended" by the hype surrounding global warming. His words of criticism and caution offer a thoughtful ending to this chapter:

> I do not oppose environmentalism. I do not oppose the political positions of either party. However, global warming, [that is] climate change, is not about environmentalism or politics. It is not a religion. It is not something you "believe in." It is science; the science of meteorology. . . . Global warming is a non-event, a manufactured crisis, and a total scam. . . . There is no runaway climate change. The impact of humans on climate is not catastrophic. Our planet is not in peril.
>
> In time . . . the outrageous scam will be obvious. As the temperature rises, polar ice cap melting, coastal flooding, and super storm pattern all fail to occur as predicted, everyone will come to realize we have been duped. . . . Natural cycles and drifts in climate are as much if not more responsible for any climate changes underway. I strongly believe that the next twenty years are equally as likely to see a cooling trend as they are to see a warming trend.

Global warming. It is the hoax. It is bad science. It is a high-jacking of public policy. It is no joke. It is the greatest scam in history.

Is Coleman correct? Thousands of people believe that he is, but thousands of others don't. In any case, he does not know for sure; none of us do. For an issue as important as possible changing climates, it is very important to weigh *all* evidence. Our very future is at stake.

THE HUMAN RESPONSE

Today, everyone seems to be concerned about global warming. Most people wonder what can and should be done to protect the environment and future human well-being. As you have learned in reading this book, there are countless options from which to select! In most instances, recommendations boil down to "should we do this?" or "should we do that?" counterproposals.

Many people believe that we must cut back on the use of fossil fuels—NOW! There are even a number of suggestions that are too far-fetched to discuss here, including scrubbing the atmosphere or reducing incoming solar radiation. The problem with many of the suggestions is that they would do far more harm than good. Let's look at some of the major proposed responses to possible climate change to see what their consequences would be.

UNITED NATIONS CLIMATE CHANGE CONFERENCES

Certainly you have heard of the Kyoto (Japan, 1997) and Copenhagen (Denmark, 2009) conferences. They were organized by the United Nations. Both conferences established accords (agreements) and protocols (rules, or guidelines) by which all countries are supposed to abide. The results, however, set goals that few countries actually intend to meet, or, for that matter, could if they tried.

The Kyoto Conference

According to the Kyoto accords, by 2012 levels of greenhouse gas emissions must be 20 percent lower than they were in 1997. (In reality, today's emissions are somewhat higher than they were a decade ago.) If one believes the media hype, the treaty's goal is to sharply reduce global greenhouse gas emissions and thereby lessen the threat of global warming. There are, however, a growing number of critics. Some experts believe that, even if fully implemented, the protocols would have very little if any effect on CO_2 emissions or Earth's temperature. The costs, however, would be astronomical, amounting to trillions of dollars.

For some observers, it has been quite clear from the outset that the Kyoto Treaty has little to do with global warming. Rather it was implemented to achieve a hidden agenda, a goal much different from its expressed purpose. In this context, it is important to know that the United Nations is dominated by developing countries. If fully implemented, the Kyoto Treaty would result in a massive transfer of wealth. Billions of dollars would be paid by industrial countries to poorer non-industrial nations. Naturally, representatives of poor countries gleefully support such a program. Few people realize that under the guidelines, industrial countries could go right on polluting. They simply would pay poor countries for the right to do so. Environmental benefits, some suggest, would be almost nonexistent.

Today, the global economic engine is powered by fossil fuels. Few people seem to recognize how important this is. What would happen if, for example, their use was drastically reduced? Without alternative sources of cheap energy, the global economy would crumble.

There is a very important lesson to be learned from history—when the economy of developed countries fails, it is the poor who suffer the greatest pain. This is true whether the poverty occurs within regions or countries, or among individuals.

Certainly the effects of diminished economic productivity would have an enormous impact on economic growth and development in the world's industrial nations. This is why the

Demonstrators protest the Kyoto Treaty before a climate summit in 2001. Despite its commitment to the environment, the United States has refrained from signing the treaty.

United States has not signed the Kyoto Treaty. Several countries, including India and the heavily polluting and rapidly growing economic giant China, signed but are exempt from abiding by the treaty. Within the United States, nonparticipation in the Kyoto accord has become a hot political issue. During the George W. Bush presidency, Democrats heaped criticism on his administration for not supporting the Kyoto agreement. On this issue, however, memories seem to be rather short. The Kyoto Treaty was adopted in 1997, at which time a Democrat, Bill Clinton, was president. Further, the Senate voted 95–0 *against* U.S. ratification of the treaty. Both political parties unanimously agreed that the Kyoto Treaty was not in the country's best interest.

The Copenhagen Conference

In December 2009, another United Nations climate change conference was held in Copenhagen, Denmark. Among the 15,000 in attendance were heads of state, advisers, diplomats, journalists, and others. One group, however, was noticeably absent from the conference: scientists! This was a political, rather than scientific, gathering. Climate change, itself, seemed to be a minor concern. Rather, climate change was used as a political tool to achieve other goals. In this context, it is important to know that most of the countries represented at the conference are poor.

From the outset, the conference appeared to have two primary goals. First, the agenda focused upon development of a system whereby countries that produce large quantities of CO_2 emissions would be penalized. Many critics saw this as a penalty for economic success imposed by poor countries upon the rich. If implemented, the system would lay the foundation for a massive transfer of wealth from developed to less developed nations. Second, the agenda called for the establishment of a global emissions task force. Legally binding quotas would be established, with which countries must abide. Emissions would be measured, and nations that broke the rules would be penalized. A number of countries worried that this would lay the foundation for a one-world government. If adopted, they believed that they would begin to lose their sovereignty (independence).

Overall, the conference failed to agree upon most of its goals. In regard to greenhouse gas emissions, it reached a rather toothless, nonbinding agreement. Rich countries are supposed to voluntarily list emissions targets. Poor countries simply should tell what actions they intend to take in order to reduce global warming pollution. A financial agreement, however, was reached. Rich nations agreed to provide $30 billion in emergency climate aid to poor countries between 2010 and 2012. The document also set a goal of providing $100 billion a year to poor countries by 2020. While this agreement may have little to do with climate change, it does have a rather positive side. The funds will help poor countries develop their economies and thereby improve the lives of their citizens.

ENERGY AND CULTURE

In 1949, anthropologist Leslie A. White published a paper in which he presented a very interesting theory. Professor White suggested that culture (everything humans know, have, and are able to do) advances in response to per capita energy consumption. Subsequent studies have shown his theory to be correct. (You can judge for yourself. Compare country rankings of energy consumption and human well-being as they appear on the following Web sites: http://en.wikipedia.org/wiki/List_of_countries_by_energy_consumption_per_capita and http://en.wikipedia.org/wiki/List_of_countries_by_Human_Development_Index.)

Since the beginning of the Industrial Revolution more than two centuries ago, the world's economic growth has depended upon fossil fuels. Today, 85 percent of all energy produced in the United States comes from petroleum, coal, and natural gas. Half of the country's electricity alone is generated by coal-powered plants. Nearly all transportation—whether motor vehicle, rail, or ship—depends upon petroleum. Imagine how different your life would be without such mobility. How would you get to the various places you visit on a regular basis? How would the stores where you shop get their merchandise? How would public service vehicles—the police cars, fire trucks, ambulances, and others—get to their destinations when desperately needed? How would garbage and other trash be picked up and dumped? The list goes on and on, but you get the idea.

MAKING CONNECTIONS

HOW WOULD YOU SPEND THE MONEY?

Now that you have a better grasp of the issues related to global warming, it is time for your "final exam." One set of experts tells us that the damage from anthropogenic global warming will result in trillions of dollars in losses. To reduce the amount of greenhouse gases placed in the atmosphere will also cost trillions of dollars. Alternative energy sources must be discovered or developed. And huge adjustments must be made in the way the global economy works. Yet other experts tell us that Earth's recent warming is perfectly natural. We simply have been on the warm part of a normal climate cycle. Money spent trying to stop global warming, they argue, is money wasted.

Imagine that you hold a position of major global leadership as head of a powerful organization with, say, $100 billion to spend. The only condition is that the money must be spent on projects that will be most beneficial to humankind. It is within your power to decide how and where the money will be spent. How would you spend the money in such a way as to bring the greatest benefit to people, countries, and the global environment? Would you spend it on global warming-related matters or on other problems that you believe to be of greater importance to the well-being of humanity? Either way, list as many projects as possible and indicate how humanity would benefit from your generosity.

During the past three decades, China's economy has experienced average annual growth of almost 10 percent. About two-thirds of the country's energy is generated by coal. Certainly its dependence upon coal will continue for decades to come. China's coal reserves rank right behind those of the United States and Russia. During recent years, China, on average, has opened two new coal-fired plants each week. Because of its heavy dependence on coal, the country is a major contributor to atmospheric CO_2. According to one estimate, if China's use of coal increases as it has since 1980, by 2030 it will be spewing out as much CO_2 as is the *entire world* today! India and a number of economically developing countries also depend upon coal as their primary source of energy. Should those countries be denied the opportunity to grow economically?

Many people would like to see the world's economy and energy consumption slow down. But how realistic is this idea? As the world became painfully aware during the Great Depression of the 1930s, "As goes the U.S. economy, so goes the world's economy." This is a lesson that is being learned again during the current global economic downturn. The American economy is the source of energy that powers the global economic engine. In the context of global connections, none is more closely interwoven than is the global economy.

AN IMPORTANT LESSON

There is a very important lesson to be learned from the global warming debate: It is essential that citizens become well informed on important issues. Far too much of what we hear or read comes from biased sources (on both sides of the issue and political fence). People and organizations with their own agendas want you to believe *their* way and therefore tell you how and what to think. As an educated person, you must look at all sides of any important issue. This is particularly true in regard to something as important as the possibility of changing climates. Basically, we first must ask, is Earth actually warming? Second, if the temperature is warming, is it rising at an unusually rapid rate? Third, if warming is occurring, are humans or natural cycles responsible? Finally, in the absence of concrete knowledge, is it wise to spend several trillion dollars to stop something that may not exist?

IT'S UP TO YOU

There is no consensus among scientists that added atmospheric CO_2 is causing temperatures to warm. During the past decade the concentration of carbon dioxide has continued to increase. Temperatures, however, have gradually decreased during this period. Earth's average temperature is 59°F (15°C). Despite what you might read or hear to the contrary, every year since 1998 has been cooler than average. In fact, the global temperature in 2008 was the coolest in four decades, and this cooling trend continued during 2009. It certainly is true that many scientists continue to believe in anthropogenic global warming. But many do not, as is illustrated by the nearly 31,500 who have signed the Petition Project. According to a recent U.S. Senate Minority report, more than 650 scientists who were once AGW believers have now become skeptics. And their number is growing rapidly. At this time, no scientist can say with certainty that it *is* happening because of human activity. If one is to be honest, all he or she can say in regard to AGW is that "based on *my* interpretation of the evidence, *I believe* that . . ."

As you look to the future—hopefully with an open mind—you need to approach the subject of global warming in a nonbiased way. Both the Bibliography and Further Reading sections contain many sources that present both sides of the global warming issue. It is hoped that you will learn more about what both sides have to say on the matter of AGW. Then it will be up to you to decide for yourself what you believe is or is not happening and why. What do you think? The future, after all, is yours!

GLOSSARY

anthropogenic   Caused by human activity.

climate   The average weather over a long time period.

climatologist   Scientist who studies climates.

culture   Everything that humans know, possess, and are able to do because we are human.

ecology   The relationships between living organisms and the environment in which they live.

ecosystem   A set of ecological relationships that give rise to a particular ecological system, such as a desert or tropical rain forest.

feedback   Any process that alters climatic changes that are already underway, either by increasing them (positive feedback) or suppressing them (negative feedback).

global warming   In current popular use, it refers to anthropogenic warming of the planet believed by some to be caused by the addition of carbon dioxide (CO_2) to the atmosphere.

greenhouse effect   Various gases within the atmosphere act like a blanket, causing the lower atmosphere to be warmer. They include water vapor, carbon dioxide, and methane.

habitat   The environment in which a plant or animal can survive.

meteorologist   Scientist who studies weather.

paleoclimatology   The study of ancient climates by using rocks, sediments, glacial action, tree rings, and other surrogate indicators of climate and climate change.

paleontologist   Scientist who studies ancient life, often based upon fossils.

precipitation   Any form of falling moisture, including rain, snow, hail, and sleet.

weather   Day-to-day condition of the atmosphere.

BIBLIOGRAPHY

Berger, A., and M.F. Loutre. "An Exceptionally Long Interglacial Ahead?" *Science* 23 (August 23, 2002): pp. 1287–1288.

Burroughs, William J. *Climate Change: A Multidisciplinary Approach.* Cambridge and New York: Cambridge University Press, 2001.

Climate Change: State of Knowledge. Washington, DC: Office of Science and Technology Policy, 1997.

Coleman, John. "The Amazing Story Behind the Global Warming Scam." KUSI-TV (January 29, 2009). Available online. http://www.kusi.com/weather/colemanscorner/38574742.html (accessed 6/22/09).

Global Warming Petition Project. Available online. http://www.petitionproject.org/.

Imbrie, John, and K.P. Imbrie. *Ice Ages: Solving the Mystery.* Cambridge, Mass.: Harvard University Press, 2005.

"Is There Global Cooling?" Available online. http://www.isthereglobalcooling.com/.

"List of Countries by Energy Consumption Per Capita," Wikipedia.com. Available online. http://en.wikipedia.org/wiki/List_of_countries_by_energy_consumption_per_capita.

"List of Countries by Human Development Index," Wikipedia.com. Available online. http://en.wikipedia.org/wiki/List_of_countries_by_Human_Development_Index.

Lomborg, Bjorn. *Cool It: The Skeptical Environmentalist's Guide to Global Warming.* New York: Alfred A. Knopf, 2008.

Mann, Michael E., and Lee R. Kump. *Dire Predictions, Understanding Global Warming: The Illustrated Guide to the Findings of the IPCC.* New York: DK Publishing Inc., 2009.

Morano, Marc. "New Peer-Reviewed Scientific Studies Chill Global Warming Fears." U.S. Senate Committee on Environment and Public Works: Minority Page. Press Release, August 20, 2007.

Nova, Joanne. "The Skeptic's Handbook." http://joannenova.com.au/global-warming/ (2009).

Philander, S. George, ed. *Encyclopedia of Global Warming and Climate Change.* Thousand Oaks, Calif.: Sage Publishers, 2008.

Ruddiman, William F. *Earth's Climate: Past and Future.* New York: W.H. Freeman and Company, 2008.

Singer, S. Fred, ed. *Nature, Not Human Activity, Rules the Climate: Summary for Policymakers of the Report of the Nongovernmental Panel on Climate Change.* Chicago: The Heartland Institute, 2008.

Singer, S. Fred, and Dennis Avery. *Unstoppable Global Warming: Every 1,500 Years.* Lanham, Md.: Rowman & Littlefield Publishers, Inc., 2008.

Watts, Anthony. *Is the U.S. Surface Temperature Record Reliable?* Chicago: The Heartland Institute, 2009.

White, Leslie A. "Energy and the Evolution of Culture," in *The Science of Culture.* New York: Farrar, Straus and Company, 1949, pp. 363–393.

Zeng, Ning, Yihui Ding, et al. "Climate Change—The Chinese Challenge," *Science* 319 (February 8, 2008): pp. 730–731.

 # FURTHER RESOURCES 

Bily, Cynthia A., ed. *Global Warming: Opposing Viewpoints.* Farmington Hills, Mich.: Greenhaven Press, 2006.

Gore, Albert. *An Inconvenient Truth: The Planetary Emergency of Global Warming and What We Can Do About It.* Emmaus, Pa.: Rodale Press, 2006.

Gritzner, Charles F. *Feeding a Hungry World.* New York: Chelsea House Publishers, 2009.

Gritzner, Charles F. *The Human Population.* New York: Chelsea House Publishers, 2009.

Horner, Christopher C. *Red Hot Lies: How Global Warming Alarmists Use Threats, Fraud, and Deception to Keep You Misinformed.* Washington, DC: Regnery Publishing Inc., 2008.

Pavlović, Zoran. *Changing Global Economy.* New York: Chelsea House Publishers, 2009.

Spencer, Roy W. *Climate Confusion: How Global Warming Hysteria Leads to Bad Science, Pandering Politicians, and Misguided Policies That Hurt the Poor.* New York and London: Encounter Books, 2008.

Tennesen, Michael. *The Complete Idiot's Guide to Global Warming.* Indianapolis, Ind.: ALPHA Books, 2008.

WEB SITES

Climate Depot
http://www.climatedepot.com

Intergovernmental Panel on Climate Change (IPCC)
http://www.ipcc.ch/

JoNova skeptic's Web Site
http://joannenova.com.au/

National Oceanic and Atmospheric Administration, National Climatic Data Center, "Global Warming: Frequently Asked Questions"
http://www.ncdc.noaa.gov/oa/climate/globalwarming.html

U. S. Environmental Protection Agency, "Climate Change"
http://www.epa.gov/climatechange/index.html

United States Senate Committee on Environment and Public Works
http://epw.senate.gov/public/index.cfm

World Climate Research Program
http://wcrp.wmo.int/wcrp-index.html

INDEX

 # PICTURE CREDITS 

 # ABOUT THE AUTHOR 

CHARLES F. GRITZNER is Distinguished Professor of Geography Emeritus at South Dakota State University. He retired after 50 years of college teaching and now looks forward to what he hopes to be many more years of research and writing. Gritzner has served as both president and executive director of the National Council for Geographic Education and has received the council's highest honor, the George J. Miller Award for Distinguished Service to Geographic Education, as well as other honors from the NCGE, the Association of American Geographers, and other organizations.